MW01610979

Don't Be Afraid...
Said the Lord

By John Grady

"Don't Be Afraid" Said the Lord
Revised Edition
By John Grady

PRINTED BY: KDP, an Amazon.com company
AUTHOR'S EMAIL: johngradysecurity@gmail.com

Bookcover: Dave Kerby
Editing: Sandra Grady

ISBN: 978-0-9688955-7-3

DEDICATION

To my wife, Sandra. What an incredible encourager, supporter and editor. Your suggestions were so valued, needed and appreciated. Thank you for your love and support.

To our granddaughters Katie and Ellie that you will become all HE has purposed for you and may you each fulfill HIS calling for your lives.
To the many who have deposited the ways of HIS Kingdom into my life and have stood with me in my spiritual journey.

To my parents, Cyril and Margaret Grady who helped make me into who I am, in spite of myself.

To you HOLY SPIRIT for your challenge, encouragement, inspiration, counsel and anointing so the name of JESUS and our FATHER may be glorified.

ABOUT THE AUTHOR

John Grady, CPP has traveled to over 50 Countries around the world and has spoken at Conferences, Churches, Business meetings and as a guest on Christian Television.

John has served on a number of Board of Directors and numerous Advisory Boards which include the Billy Graham Evangelical Crusade in Vancouver, World Wide Pictures "The Prodigal ", ICCC Canada a National marketplace ministry and one of the Canadian hosts to the Jewish survivors of the 1939 St. Louis ship. John has hosted and attended Government Prayer breakfasts throughout North America in honoring and praying for Government officials.

John has authored a biblical based book on The Heart, as well as Travel Security and Safety Awareness and Counter Terrorism

Threat Assessment. John is a former member of the Royal Canadian Mounted Police (RCMP) and is an Internationally recognized Security Professional with a Certified Professional Designation (CPP). John has been honored several times internationally for his leadership in the Security Profession as well as having an Annual Award being presented in his name for special service in the protection of life and property.

INTRODUCTION

While reading scripture when the LORD speaks to heroes of our faith such as Abram (Abraham), Jacob, Moses, David, Nehemiah, Daniel, Zechariah, Mary, John, Paul, Peter and others with the words "Do not be Afraid" it should cause us to examine whether those words apply only to the lives of the Patriarchs as well as the early church fathers of do they apply to us as well.

For example, are you similar to one of the Biblical figures identified in this book who inspires, perseveres, leads, influences, mentors or are you a peacemaker, merciful, visionary or faithful?

If we believe fear paralyses then what is the difference, if any between men of fear versus men of faith? Is it possible that we unknowingly have fear in our lives, such as fear of failure, finances, being judged, health, acceptance, change, loneliness, future, correction, rejection and so on?
When GOD is about to do something significant that involves us knowing what is about to take

place, in HIS love HE can prepare us with these words, "Do not be Afraid". The biblical characters heard those words from the LORD and at times we need to as well. As you read this book try to identify yourself with one of the biblical characters referred to or their circumstances.

This book is meant to encourage you to help recognize what you are going through, to allow the HOLY SPIRIT to minister healing and freedom so that the LORD can fulfill HIS purposes and calling for your life.

We know from scripture that perfect love casts out fear and that perfect love is found only in HIM. That comes out of true intimacy with OUR LORD so that our faith and obedience to HIM are fulfilled. I trust you will be able to identify with the numerous other bible characters who had these words spoken to them! "Do not be Afraid" said the LORD.

ABRAHAM

After this, the Word of the LORD came to Abram in a vision: "Do not be Afraid, Abram. I am your shield, your very great reward."

Genesis 15: 1

Abram is an incredible man of GOD who should encourage all of us in our journey of walking with GOD in obedience to the LORD. As you examine the story of Abram you can see the special relationship between Abram and the LORD and can't help but be in awe of not only the faith of Abram but also the faithfulness of our LORD in not only dealing with Abram but revealing to us how faithful HE is and how HE desires to walk with us in our walk with HIM.

Abram is a Patriarch of our faith and is known as a "father of all who believe" who walks in obedience to the voice of the LORD with Abram leaving his people and his father's household in the Haran to go to a land that the LORD would show him, which as we know is Canaan but of course Abram did not know. Think about it – what faith. We have problems leaving anywhere without our GPS let alone going in faith to a foreign land without first knowing all the details and potential issues that need to be covered beforehand and even then, most of us would not walk in faith as Abram did.

The promise the LORD made to Abram is that the LORD would make him into a great nation, the LORD would bless him and make Abram's name great and Abram would be a blessing. I don't think our spiritual biographies look too good beside Abram's but let's remember in his humanness Abram told his wife Sarai to pretend to be his sister as he was scared for his own life when they eventually arrived in Egypt because of the famine in Canaan and later at Gerar with King Abimelech. There are not many husbands who would give up their wife as a sister to protect their own life as Abram did and yet we see the LORD interceding in these matters. As we examine Abram's life, we see that he allowed the LORD to make him into the man of GOD that he became and that must encourage all of us.

It is important for us to remember the genealogy of JESUS CHRIST and the connection to Abraham:

Matthew 1:1-2 A record of the genealogy of JESUS CHRIST the son of David, the son of Abraham: Abraham was the father of Isaac, Isaac the father of Jacob, Jacob the father of Judah and his brothers.

Matthew 1:6 and Jesse the father of King David. David was the father of Solomon, whose mother had been Uriah's wife.

Matthew 1: 17 Thus there were fourteen generations in all from Abraham to David, fourteen from David to the exile to Babylon, and fourteen from the exile to the CHRIST.

Abram, after leaving Egypt eventually settled at Hebron and was a wealthy man. In fact, Abram told the King of Sodom that he would accept nothing from the King so the King would never be able to say that he had made Abram rich. Sadly, most of us can say it is the LORD who gives us blessings, but it can just be the right thing to say when we really do not have a full understanding of the LORD'S favor such as Abram acknowledged.

The story of Abram is about to change:

After this, the word of the LORD cam to Abram in a vision: "Do not be Afraid, Abram. I am your shield, your very great reward. Genesis 15:1

So, th e question is, why is the LORD now telling Abram "Do not be Afraid." Does it not pertain to us also and what we are to learn from what the LORD is about to teach Abram and us. As you read on in the story of Abram, we realize that the LORD is about to make major changes through testing of Abram.

Do we embrace the words change or testing and if not, are we missing out in what the LORD desires for us? In our natural make up it is safe to state that we resist change or new beginnings, but as we receive HIM by HIS SPIRIT, we should choose to live in the supernatural to walk in HIS will and power.

What is enlightening is Abram's response to the vision and the LORD'S handling of both Abram and the response of Abram. Abram, like most of us, had a deep unresolved matter that had been really bothering him and in spite of the deep foundational truth the LORD has spoken to Abram, we find Abram first bypassing the LORD'S word to him so he can get his deep issue tabled. Abram and his wife are getting well on in their age and are childless. In their culture at that time, it was a major issue. Just to make sure the LORD gets the picture; Abram lets the LORD know his servant is going to inherit everything. The LORD did not give Abram a long theology lesson but met Abram where he was at and the HOLY SPIRIT does the same with us today. The LORD reveals to Abram that he will father a son and HE takes Abram outside and shows Abram the stars and confirms Abram's inheritance. Abram believed the Lord, and HE credited it to him as righteousness. End of the matter, right? It is one thing to believe and it is another to walk it out. It is in the walking it out that the words "Do not be Afraid" become the words of faith because the LORD was revealing calling, inheritance and destiny. What has the LORD revealed to you about your calling, your inheritance and your destiny?

The LORD confirms to Abram and also to us three important fundamental issues from Genesis 15:1:

1. "Do not be Afraid". The LORD is about to do something, and Abram needs to be free of fear. We too must be set free of fear in order for the LORD to fulfill HIS plans for our life.

2. The LORD, and only the LORD, is Abram's shield, and that is also important for us to remember. The LORD is our shield, our fortress, our deliverer and our protection.

3. The LORD is Abram's very great reward, and in our jargon the LORD is really the motivation and purpose of our life and subsequently our reward. Without the LORD, we have nothing. Our purposes and life on earth are measured in the LORD.

We see in Abram's walk, major key events that should encourage us as Abram matured into the man of GOD:

The first is helping Abram and us to fully understand the truth of the word from the LORD so HE goes out of HIS way to introduce to Abram and to us a Covenant which is that when the LORD makes a promise in spite of anything, HE will keep HIS promise (Covenant). Every time we see a rainbow in the sky we can remember the Covenant the LORD made with Noah and always be encouraged of HIS faithfulness. Unfortunately, today the word covenant is tossed around loosely but in the LORD it means unbreakable.

The second event with Abram, we learn something some of us can relate to and that is going ahead of the LORD and assuming we are fulfilling HIS promise. In Abram's case, it was agreeing to sleep with Hagar, the consequence being the birth of Ishmael, which of course was not the LORD'S will. Being a doer, it is easy to begin a project the LORD has revealed to us, but we need to also understand the timing. We need to ensure we also have the timing of the LORD, so we are working with HIM. If you are not a doer for the LORD of HIS will then isn't it time to get out of the boat.

The third event was when the LORD began the deep work of changing Abram's name to Abraham and for his wife Sarai to be renamed Sarah and miraculously in time the birth of Isaac takes place which is the start of the heirs and promises of the LORD to Abraham. Abraham was 99 when the LORD reminded him of HIS Covenant and of course Abraham initially laughed at the thought of being a father at 100 years of and Sarah giving birth at 90 years of age.

The fourth event is the intercession of Abraham over the people living at Sodom and Gomorrah. The LORD was about to judge Sodom and Gomorrah and Abraham interceded to the point that if there were ten righteous people in Sodom the LORD agreed he would not destroy the city. Just think how history could have been changed if there were ten righteous. What city and or Country are you and I interceding for?

The fifth event is the willingness and obedience of Abraham to sacrifice his son Isaac because of his incredible faith and trust in the LORD. For some of us who have problems relating to both the request from the LORD and Abrahams willing faith and trust at the request of the LORD it can help us understand the love of the FATHER for us and the giving of HIS SON, JESUS CHRIST as sacrifice for our sins and the price JESUS paid in our relationship HE desired with us. We need to understand what Abraham's obedience to the LORD meant to the LORD which is found in:

Genesis 22: 15-18 The angel of the LORD called to Abraham from heaven a second time and said, "I swear by myself, declares the LORD, that because you have done this and have not withheld your son, your only son, I will surely bless you and make your descendants as numerous as the stars in the sky and as the sand on the seashore. Your descendants will take possession of the cities of their enemies, and through your offspring all nations on earth will be blessed, BECAUSE you have OBEYED ME."

I find it most interesting that the LORD has Abraham look heavenward to the stars and for those of us who repent to the LORD and receive HIM we are looking forward to living in eternity in Heaven with HIM an yet having Abraham looking down in the ground as it is in the dust where the LORD GOD formed man while breathing into the nostrils the breath of life.

Upon reviewing the journey of Abraham, we can see why the LORD made the statement of "Don't be Afraid." We should be encouraged and challenged by the work of GOD in the life of Abraham.

What is the vision the LORD has given you and can you, like Abraham, discuss it with the LORD so you can believe HIM for it? And remember the words to Abraham: "Do not be Afraid."

HAGAR

Genesis 21: 17-18 GOD heard the boy crying and the angel of GOD called to Hagar from heaven and said to her, "What is the matter, Hagar? Do not be Afraid; GOD has heard the boy crying as he lies there. Lift the boy up and take him by the hand, for I will make him into a great nation.

Hagar enters into our biblical picture as an Egyptian maidservant to Abraham's wife Sarah who was barren and also after the LORD has given a promise to Abraham that an heir would come from his own body. With Sarah still barren she decides to help the LORD fulfill HIS promise and suggests to Abraham that he sleep with Hagar which he agrees to so that they could build a family through Hagar. So often we too try and help the LORD in something HE has promised but yet not fulfilled. Disastrous consequences are about to happen to the three individuals. Hagar becomes pregnant and begins to despise Sarah; Sarah begins to mistreat Hagar and Abraham washes his hands of the matter. Hagar flees from the family and an angel of the LORD finds Hagar near a spring in the desert and tells her to go back to Sarah and to submit to her. The angel of the LORD shares with Hagar that Hagar's descendants would be too numerous to count and that the child she is carrying is a son and is to be named Ishmael (which means GOD hears) and gives her a future behaviour pattern of Ishmael. You can imagine the impact this has on Hagar and she states that "I have now seen the ONE who sees me". Hagar returns and gives birth to Ishmael but the promise of the LORD to Abraham and Sarah takes place and Sarah becomes pregnant and gives birth to the heir, Isaac.

After giving birth to Isaac, Sarah saw there were problems with Hagar and Ishmael, so she instructs Abraham to get rid of the two of them. The LORD speaks to Abraham and confirms to him to listen to what Sarah is stating because it is through Isaac that his offspring will be reckoned. HE also tells Abraham that HE will make Ishmael (Abraham's offspring) into a nation also. It is amazing for those of us in the 21st Century to be able to look back at history, dysfunction and sin to see how it has played out over the years and the years to come.

Hagar and Ishmael are on their way and arrive in the desert of Beersheba now without water. She places Ishmael under one of the bushes and begins to sob believing he was going to die, forgetting and or not believing the promise GOD had made to her. Does not that happen to us as well? GOD'S word, faithfulness and mercy come to the forefront not only for Hagar and for Ishmael but to help us to get to really know we can really trust HIM.

Genesis 21: 17-18 GOD heard the boy crying and the angel of GOD called to Hagar from heaven and said to her, "What is then matter, Hagar? Do not be Afraid; GOD has heard the boy crying as he lies there. Lift the boy up and take him by the hand, for I will make him into a great nation."

GOD opened her eyes and by "coincidence" she saw a well of water and the LORD was with Ishmael as he grew up and eventually Hagar found a wife for him from Egypt. The rest is history.

It becomes clear to us why the LORD spoke the words "Do not be Afraid" to Hagar as it was not just to save the lives of her and her son BUT it was the LORD watching over HIS promise to fulfill it and if we will also not walk in doubt and fear to the promises of the LORD to us they also will be fulfilled.

ISAAC

Genesis 26:24 That night the LORD appeared to him and said, "I am the GOD of your father Abraham, Do not be Afraid, for I am with you: I will bless you and will increase the number of your descendants for the sake of my servant Abraham."

Isaac is certainly a miracle boy with his parents, Abraham at the age of 100 being the father and his mother Sarah giving birth to him at 90 years of age. No wonder Abraham and Sarah both giggled when the LORD made the promise to them a year earlier. The promise however was bigger than Isaac as it was a Covenant given to Abraham and of course included Isaac as the heir to Abraham and Sarah. So often our vision is that we see one miracle, but the LORD is looking so much further and sees miracle after miracle after miracle to bring HIS purposes and Kingdom into fulfillment.

Have you ever considered how Isaac felt when at the age of 16 his father Abraham took him on a little trip where he placed the wood for the burnt offering on Isaac while Abraham carried the fire and knife and then placed Isaac on the altar on top of the wood and took his knife and was about to slay Isaac. As we know an angel of the LORD then spoke to Abraham telling him not to lay a hand on Isaac and spoke the key words "now I know that you fear GOD because you have not withheld from me your son, your only son" and by "coincidence" Abraham looked up and he saw a ram in a thicket caught by its thorns. Isaac must have wondered what was going on during this process to ask his father where the lamb for the burnt offering was. You have to wonder when Isaac being released from the altar and after they had sacrificed the ram how Abraham and Isaac discussed this matter and how Isaac would have felt with any explanation Abraham offered. Did it have an impact on Isaac; did Isaac ever wonder what could be next?

Isaac was 40 years old when he married Rebekah and just like Isaac's parents Rebekah was barren but in answer to prayer and God's purposes Rebekah became pregnant with twins with the LORD telling her that the older, Esau would serve the younger, Jacob. We also see a similar pattern of Isaac like his father Abraham when the famine took place at Gerar stating that his wife Rebekah was his sister "because he was afraid to say, she is my wife "and thought he might lose his life on account of her beauty. WOW. What is that expression "like father like son?" Like his father Abraham he clearly had fear for his own life, and their survival patterns were identical of offering up their wives as their sisters.

When you read the beginning of Chapter 26, you will see that the LORD appeared to Isaac and wanted him to stay in the land. The LORD confirmed that HE would be with Isaac. HE would bless him, and his descendants would receive the land. The LORD once again confirms the oath HE swore to Isaac's father Abraham, which of course is known as the Abrahamic Covenant.

Isaac stayed in the land, became very wealthy and subsequently got in a water and land dispute with the Philistines. If this was just an issue of victory over the land and water, all the LORD needed to say was something like, don't worry, I am in control, and I will give you victory, but I believe it was much deeper and is relevant for us today.

In Genesis 26: 24, the LORD repeated to Isaac who HE was, and because of HIS covenant with Abraham, HE would bless Isaac and increase the number of Isaac's descendants. What the LORD added to Isaac were these key words, "Do not be Afraid, for I am with you."

We also need to learn to identify who we are in CHRIST and what that really means. Just as Isaac needed the comfort of "Do not be Afraid" he also needed to better understand this Covenant making GOD and Isaac's personal relationship with HIM. Because we walk and live in the New Covenant there are certain promises and authorities that we have received, but because of the New Covenant our lives are supposed to be under HIS LORDSHIP and are no longer our own. It is imperative that we really know the Covenant making GOD we have entered into a relationship with. Isaac was a second generation follower of the LORD. Many in the church today who have been raised in the church are 2nd, 3rd or 4th generational believers in JESUS CHRIST but some have not received the reality and fullness HE has to offer. When JESUS stated, "I will never leave nor forsake you" HE meant what HE said, and we can stand on that word because it is personal and true to each and every follower of JESUS CHRIST. Let's remember that on two occasions in Genesis 26, the LORD reminded Isaac that Isaac was the inheritance of the promise to his father Abraham but on the second time in Verse 24, the LORD knew Isaac had to have the comfort and personal encouragement of the words, "Do not be Afraid." During our dark and lonely times when the enemy comes to plant doubts and fears, we must take JESUS CHRIST at HIS word to us because HE is truth.

Isaac was getting on in age and it was time for him to give his birthright blessing to his oldest son Esau. As we know Esau had sold his birthright to Jacob thinking he was going to die however to add to the matter there was a conspiracy between Isaac's wife Rebekah and their son Jacob to have

Jacob receive the blessing and not Esau. As it turns out through deception Jacob did receive the blessing from Isaac making Jacob lord over Esau, including all the relatives and servants sustaining Jacob with grain and wine. Isaac told Esau that Esau would serve his brother Jacob. Although all of these birthright events were troubling to Isaac, we must remember that the LORD had spoken to Rebekah while she was pregnant with Esau and Jacob and stated, "The older will serve the younger."

Interestingly when Abraham died both Isaac and Ishmael buried Abraham with his wife Sarah in the cave of Machpelah near Mamre.

There was something important that the LORD spoke to Isaac when HE was confirming HIS promises to Isaac which is found in Genesis 26:5 "because Abraham OBEYED ME and kept MY requirements, MY commands, MY decrees and MY laws. " Like Isaac we need to be reminded of walking in obedience to what the LORD gives us and how the LORD watches over HIS word and promises to perform them and we "Do not need to be Afraid".

JACOB

And GOD spoke to Israel in a vision at night and said, "Jacob! Jacob!"

"Here I am," he replied. "I am GOD, the GOD of your father," HE said. "Do not be Afraid to go down to Egypt, for I will make you into a great nation there."
Genesis 46: 2-3

Jacob had the most interesting journey with the reputation as the deceiver who stole his brother Esau's birthright and with Isaac his fathers blessing Jacob went to Paddan Haran to stay with Laban, the brother of Jacobs mother Rebekah, to avoid his older brother Esau. It was along the way to Paddan Haran that Jacob had a dream where the LORD introduced HIMSELF as the LORD of his grandfather Abraham and his father Isaac confirming HIS blessing upon Jacob and his offspring and that HE would return Jacob to the native land. Although Jacob was Afraid, he realized what at awesome place it was, then taking a stone that had been under his head he set it on a pillar and anointing it with oil naming the place Bethel making a vow to the LORD. Jacob had encountered the LORD for himself.

Jacob's relationship with Laban was not good with a foundation of mistrust and deceiving of each other. Part of the deception was Jacob having both Laban's daughters, Leah and Rachael as his wives.

Years later Jacob has a vision with the LORD telling him to leave Laban reminding Jacob that HE was the GOD of Bethel the place where Jacob had anointed the pillar with oil and made a vow to the LORD. Isn't the LORD so good in not complicating things even though we go out of our way to do so? On the journey back we see where Jacob was afraid of what Laban might do and also in prayer to the LORD, he acknowledges his fear of Esau. After Jacob had crossed the ford of the Jabbok sending his wives, maidservants and eleven sons ahead of him that he encounters a man wrestling with him until daybreak stating he (Jacob) would not let go until he, Jacob was blessed. Genesis 32:28 Then the man said, "Your name will no longer be Jacob but Israel because you have struggled with GOD and with men and have overcome." What a great lesson for us as believers in that there is a time when our traditional prayer time is not enough and the we need to struggle and wrestle with the LORD in prayer not letting go as HE in fact wants to speak to us but wants us to want it badly, HE knows the difference. We find Jacob making peace with Esau and going back to Bethel where the LORD re-confirms HIS promises to Jacob and lives in the land of Canaan.

As we know Jacob ultimately had 12 sons with his favorite being Joseph who at the age of 17 shares two dreams with his older brothers where he was ruling over them. They while jealous of Joseph even before the dreams ended up selling him to the Ishmaelites who took Joseph to Egypt. Joseph's brothers took Joseph's robe, dipped the robe in the blood of goats advising Jacob that his son Joseph had been devoured by some ferocious animal, sharing the robe as evidence. Jacob was devasted and deeply mourned for the loss of his son, Joseph.

Genesis 46:2-3 And GOD spoke to Israel in a vision at night and said, "Jacob! Jacob!" "Here I am," he replied. "I am GOD, the GOD of your father. "HE said. "Do not be Afraid to go down to Egypt, for I will make you into a great nation there."

Isn't it interesting that the place where GOD spoke to Jacob in a vision was Beersheba where Jacob as well as his father Isaac and his grandfather Abraham had also worshipped the LORD? In any case, the LORD identifies who HE is to Jacob relationally, that is being the GOD of Jacob's father Isaac. GOD is truly a GOD of order and communicates the key issues clearly with Jacob. Jacob was able to receive the message from the LORD because at the end of Chapter 45 Jacob had been told by his sons that Joseph was alive and was ruler of Egypt, but he did not initially believe them. However, when Jacob's sons told him everything that Joseph had said and when Jacob saw the carts that Joseph had sent to carry Jacob to Egypt the scripture states "the spirit of their father Jacob revived." We too need to be revived to be able to receive from the LORD. Hearing was not enough for Jacob but when 'he saw' he was revived, and we too need from time to time to be able to see. In fact, Jacob was leaving Canaan and on his way to Egypt with his family members which numbered seventy and had overnighted at Beersheba. So, if Jacob was already on his way to Egypt, why did the LORD need to speak to him and tell him, "Do not be afraid"? I believe that when there is something much bigger than ourselves that is about to take place, the unbelief of it can be so overwhelming that we need the comfort of those words. In this case the LORD was going to make Jacob (Israel) into a great nation in Egypt. How much bigger does it get than that and

yet it is the principle of this matter which we are to learn from. In our case maybe it is the HOLY SPIRIT telling us to move to a particular City, take a new job, adopt children, obtain further studies, serve in the church, write a book as HE is about to bless us and our descendants but there is a need for us to make the move. With the famine that was taking place we see the clear provision of the LORD and the keeping of HIS covenant to Abraham, Isaac and now Jacob. Can we trust Him unconditionally when the work HE is calling us to is so much bigger than we could even dream about? The answer is yes when HE speaks to us personally because HE will also always give us the Peace that means "Do not be Afraid."

Could Jacob (Israel) ever imagine that 430 years later the Israelites would be released by GOD HIMSELF out of Egypt? What is the legacy that the LORD can leave through us that will affect our families, friends, co-workers, and neighbours? Can we have faith to believe that HE has a bigger purpose and destiny for us than we could ever imagine? But let us remember, "Do not be Afraid."

JOSEPH

But Joseph said to them, "Don't be Afraid. Am I in the place of GOD? You intended to harm me, but GOD intended it for good to accomplish what is now being done, the saving of many lives. So then, Don't be Afraid. I will provide for you and your children." And he reassured them and spoke kindly to them.

Genesis 50: 19-21

As we know, Joseph's brothers were going to kill him out of jealousy after Joseph shared the dream he had with them and clearly, Joseph was Jacob's favourite son. The brothers decided instead of killing Joseph, to sell him to Midianite merchants for 20 shekels of silver who in turn, subsequently sold Joseph in Egypt to one of Pharaoh's officials named Potiphar who was captain of the Guard. The LORD gave Joseph great favor with Potiphar who expanded Joseph's duties until Potiphar's wife wrongly accused Joseph of attempting to sleep with her. Joseph's reward for serving Potiphar so well and not sinning was unjustly and wrongly placed in prison. Again, the LORD gave success to Joseph in prison and also gave Joseph the gift of interpretation of dreams which Joseph used to give the interpretation to the officials of the King of Egypt who were the cupbearer and the baker when the King had them placed in prison because they had offended him. Joseph had asked the two of them who he had given the interpretation of their dreams to mention to Pharaoh that he had given the interpretation as a means of getting out of prison. They did not and Joseph stays in prison two more years until Pharaoh has two dreams and the cupbearer mentions the gift of Joseph to Pharaoh and Joseph is presented to Pharaoh. You would think that by this time Joseph would gladly confirm the gifting he has but instead we can better understand why GOD had chosen Joseph. Joseph clarifies that he can not do it but GOD will give Pharaoh the answer. It is when GOD can trust us in the little things that HE can give us the bigger matters, and in this case Joseph explains the dreams to Pharaoh; that there will be seven years of great abundance in the land and then seven years of famine and gives the strategy so they may not be ruined by the famine. Pharaoh recognizes and agrees with the plan and then asks his officials: Genesis 41: 38 So Pharaoh asked them, "Can we find anyone like this man, one in whom is the SPIRIT of GOD?" As we know Joseph is placed in charge of the whole land of Egypt second only to Pharaoh. Do others recognize the SPIRIT of GOD in us?

What a journey Joseph has been walking in and I am not sure that the story of Joseph can properly be understood or felt by us unless we have gone through something of betrayal ourselves by people close to us. In Joseph's case, the LORD allowed such a deep, deep work within him by the different events in his life that Joseph was going to either get bitter or get better. We also have that choice as well.

We hear a great deal today about the need of inner healing (the wounds of our past) but if ever there was an example for us to study it is of course JESUS first and foremost as it is not just Judas that betrayed HIM, but each and every one of us.

Try and imagine Joseph in our Christian social circles in the 21st century and how we would share about this "dysfunctional brother" with no apparent family means serving time in jail. Clearly there was a Marketplace calling on Joseph's life and we need to be spiritually aware of destiny and inheritance in others in the Body of CHRIST in spite of apparent circumstances.

During the famine period many countries came to Egypt for grain. Jacob, living in Canaan, where there was also famine instructs his 10 sons (keeping his youngest Benjamin with him as he was afraid harm would come to him) to go to Egypt to buy grain. Let's remember that Jacob believed he had lost his beloved son Joseph and was not about to lose Benjamin. Who did the 10 brothers have to buy the grain from in Egypt? Nobody but Joseph, their brother whom they had sold to the Midianite merchants for 20 shekels. They did not recognize Joseph, but he not only recognized them but remembered his dream about them. Joseph develops a plan to have them bring Benjamin to him as well which takes place, and now he has all his brothers before him. Joseph makes himself known to them and asks if his father is still alive, but they were not able to answer him "because they were terrified in his presence."

But Joseph said to them, "Don't be Afraid. Am I in the place of GOD? You intended to harm me, but GOD intended it for good to accomplish what is now being done, the saving of many lives. So then, Don't be Afraid. I will provide for you and your children." And he reassured them and spoke kindly to them.
Genesis 50:19, 20, 21

As we see in Scripture the LORD uses many means to communicate to HIS children about "not being afraid", including man speaking to man. If ever there was a person who had a podium to speak to his brothers "Don't be Afraid" it was Joseph. Joseph was so sensitive that he didn't say it once but twice so that his brothers could hear him and receive the mind and words of the LORD.

Isn't it interesting that Joseph was able to explain to his brothers that "the saving of many lives" was why GOD allowed their betrayal and for us to better understand the purpose behind the betrayal of JESUS ultimately meant that HE would give HIS life to save the lives of all mankind who choose to believe in HIM and to receive HIM as SAVIOR and LORD.

What I love about Joseph is that not only had he forgiven when his brothers were full of guilt and shame, but he ministered healing to them by revealing to them and to us how GOD can and does work through HIS willing servants.   The expression, "You can't heal until you have been healed" ran through Joseph to his brothers. Joseph knew the issue was not about himself but about GOD'S intention and what GOD wanted to accomplish in the "saving of many lives" as well as bringing Israelites to Egypt to keep them for over 400 years. Isn't it unique that when JESUS was a baby his earthly parents escaped to Egypt for the protection of HIS life from Herod as a fulfillment of GOD'S word through the prophet, Hosea "Out of

Egypt I called my SON" and it was out of Egypt that the Israelites left to go to the Promised Land. There clearly was nothing but GOD'S love, provision and reassurance coming through Joseph to his brothers. For us who are going through a Joseph experience, let us look to the podium of resurrection that we too can say, "Don't be Afraid" and be an extension of the LORD'S purposes.

MOSES (Meeting GOD)

"Do not come any closer," GOD said. "Take off your sandals, for the place where you are standing is holy ground". Then HE said, "I am the GOD of your father, the GOD of Abraham, the GOD of Isaac and the GOD of Jacob". At this, Moses hid his face, because he was Afraid to look at GOD. Exodus 3:5, 6.

Moses, a Hebrew boy was born at a time when the Pharaoh of Joseph's time was long gone, but also at a time when the Israelites were increasing at a substantial number and the King of Egypt was fearful of their numbers, especially if a war broke out and they joined with one of Egypt's enemies. We all know the story of how Pharaoh ordered the killing of all Hebrew boys and of Moses mother placing her son in a basket on the Nile river and subsequently, how one of Pharaohs daughters found him and not only named him Moses but raised him as her son in Pharaoh's kingdom.

Just so we are not confused let's meet the two different Moses. To help clarify, every true follower of JESUS CHRIST is also two different people. The first is a person before receiving JESUS CHRIST as SAVIOR and LORD and we all have our personal stories that lead us to the moment when we become BORN of HIS SPIRIT, and the second is the change or Transformed person that takes place after receiving HIM. Our testimony should separate the two or if not then the expression of being BORN AGAIN has no merit and our faith is a cultural faith void of what HE did on the cross. What were you like before CHRIST and what changes have you allowed HIM to make within you after receiving HIM? Who have you told your story to of the miracle change that took place? The world is crying out to hear it and it is the same world that JESUS gave HIS life so please pray that the LORD will arrange the circumstance for you to share your evidence of true salvation.

The first Moses is a young teenager and man raised in the best of education and privileges, taught with all the opportunities afforded him, with entitlement and recognition in the Egyptian Kingdom. After Moses had grown up, he went to where his own people were working under hard labor and observed an Egyptian beating one of his own, a Hebrew. Moses looking around and seeing no one, killed the Egyptian and hid him assuming no one had seen the act only to find the next day when he tried to intercede between two Hebrew men fighting, they challenged him about his killing of the Egyptian man. Moses was afraid and fled to Midian away from Pharaoh who was now trying to kill Moses. While at a well in Midian seven daughters of Jethro, a priest, were drawing water for their father's flock and some shepherds drove them away only to have Moses come to their rescue and he ended up watering their flock for them. The daughters initially assumed he was an Egyptian, but in any case, he eventually married one of the daughters and settled into his new life caring for the flocks. You have to like this Moses minus the killing of the Egyptian and I think most guys can relate to him and his actions. It is important for us to realize that Moses, a Hebrew, had in his own strength unsuccessfully tried to fulfill

GOD'S purpose for his life with his defending of the Hebrew who was being beaten by the Egyptian. That is Moses part one.

The LORD heard the cry of the Israelites in Egypt and remembered HIS Covenant. HIS strategy is clear and thus HE introduces HIMSELF to the person of Moses while Moses was tending the flock of his father in law Jethro while at Horeb, known as the mountain of GOD. We know that GOD drew Moses to the burning bush and like us, HE draws us, but Moses to his credit explored the burning bush and we need to ensure that we respond to the prodding of the HOLY SPIRIT as well. What a way to be introduced to the LORD. The introduction of HIMSELF to Moses as the "GOD of" is very special because in each person named, HE places HIMSELF as the "GOD of". This is the start of Moses part two.

GOD revealed HIS holiness to Moses and when we submit to the LORDSHIP of JESUS CHRIST, HE always reveals HIS holiness to us as the foundation of our relationship to HIM. We should also experience this same reality, significance and awesome wonder when we are introduced to the CREATOR in a personal and intimate way when we receive HIS SON, JESUS CHRIST.

When many of us encounter JESUS CHRIST for the first time we come with guilt, baggage, shame and sin in one form or another but once we have confessed these issues and become filled with the HOLY SPIRIT, we all of a sudden desire to see CHRIST and hunger for intimacy with HIM. So did Moses as he really got to know the GOD of Abraham, Isaac and Jacob and now the GOD of Moses. Unfortunately, there are many in the Body of CHRIST who for very deep personal and historical reasons never do enter into the fullness of CHRIST and do not really truly learn to know and trust HIM in an intimate and personal way. The 18 inches from the head to the heart is such a long way but the heart is where we encounter the FAITHFUL ONE who can be fully trusted. With Moses, after encountering the Egyptian beating a fellow Hebrew, he subsequently spent 40 years in the desert being prepared to be GOD'S humble servant without even realizing it.

"Do not come any closer," GOD said. "Take off your sandals, for the place where you are standing is HOLY GROUND". Then HE said, "I am the GOD of your father, the GOD of Abraham, the GOD of Isaac and the GOD of Jacob". At this, Moses hid his face, because he was Afraid to look at GOD. Exodus 3:5, 6

Scripture states that Moses hid his face because he was Afraid to look at GOD. As we will see in Moses' maturing spiritual life that changed, as it should also in our lives.

The introduction of HIMSELF to Moses as the "GOD of" is very special because in each person named, HE places HIMSELF as the "GOD of". The LORD'S introduction of HIMSELF was so overwhelming for Moses with all his baggage that he had nothing in common with the holiness of GOD so that he hid his face because he was "Afraid to look at GOD".

The LORD lays out to Moses HIS rescue plan for HIS people in Egypt that includes Moses role in freeing them and what does Moses do that angers the LORD but lays out his excuses. What Moses offers the LORD is exactly what we offer the LORD at our conversion. NOTHING!!

Moses excuses included that no one will listen, highlighting the new Pharaoh as well as the Israelites and then Moses explains to the LORD that he was never eloquent; he was slow of speech and tongue and finishes it off with his counsel to the LORD that HE should send someone else. After teaching Moses about how Moses will use the staff the LORD agrees to let Aaron, Moses Levite brother, go with him and the LORD will put HIS words to Moses for Aaron to speak.

As we know from Scripture "The fear of the LORD is the beginning of wisdom" and Moses "was Afraid to look at GOD". Don't you admire the honesty of Moses? I think that was one of the reasons GOD in spite of HIS initial reaction had such a special affection for Moses and eventually "spoke to Moses face to face, clearly and not in riddles".

MOSES (The Red Sea)

Moses answered the people, "Do not be Afraid. Stand firm and you will see the deliverance the LORD will bring you today. The Egyptians you see today you will never see again. The LORD will fight for you; you need only to be still."
Exodus 14:13, 14

As we know from the word, Moses, his family and Aaron return to Egypt and they first meet with the elders of the Israelites, explaining to them what the LORD has shared with Moses, which they accepted. Moses and Aaron then went to Pharaoh to lay out the request from the LORD and as we know eventually after plagues upon plagues Pharaoh agreed to let the Hebrews go.

Interestingly the Israelite people lived in Egypt for 430 years and at the end of that time to the very day all the Hebrews left.

By day the LORD went ahead of them in a pillar of cloud to guide them on their way and at night time by a pillar of fire which gave them light so that they were able to travel both at daylight and at night. The LORD was very specific on HIS instructions to MOSES of where the Israelites were to camp which was between Migdol and the Red Sea with the LORD knowing that Pharaoh would pursue the Israelites.

Our world is crying out for leaders on one hand and ready to judge and condemn them on the other hand. Oh, the joy of leadership! Let's put this setting into perspective. Under the LORD'S instructions, Moses encamped the Israelites at the Red Sea and behind them is Pharaoh, King of Egypt with six hundred of the best chariots along with all the other chariots in Egypt with officers over all of them, along with his army who are marching towards the Israelites. We must also remember that GOD did not lead them on the road through the Philistine country which was shorter. For GOD said, "If they face war, they might change their minds and return to Egypt." (*Exodus 13:17)*. There were two options for the Israelites except for GOD:

1. Fight and be defeated and return to Egypt as slaves
2. Jump into the Red Sea and drown.

The grumbling of the Israelites was well underway when Moses makes this incredible statement to the Israelites:

Moses answered the people, "Do not be Afraid. Stand firm and you will see the deliverance the LORD will bring you today. The Egyptians you see today you will never see again. The LORD will fight for you; you need only to be still." Exodus 14:13, 14

The people could have never heard the rest of what Moses had to say unless Moses as leader was given an authority and confidence of who he was in GOD. As leaders we must also recognize the condition and state of the people we are leading and address them where they are at and not where we think they should be. It is important as a principle that what Moses stated was a clear word from the LORD because by this time of walking with the LORD Moses knew the LORD was going to deliver HIS people so that:

1. The LORD would be glorified
2. The Egyptians would know that the deliverer was the LORD. Moses knew in part, and stated in part, but his message was accurate.

True spiritual leadership comes out of intimacy with our GOD and out of that intimacy comes the anointing. Many want the anointing today but do not pay the price of true intimacy.

So often in our spiritual journeys when we are between a rock and a hard place we look for every back or side door or decide to give up and go back to Egypt. Being still is the hardest thing for many of us to do and yet sometimes we must through intimacy of walking in the SPIRIT know that:

1. The LORD will be the deliverer and thus glorified
2. HE will be revealing HIMSELF to those who do not know HIM.

The events at the Red Sea are clearly remembered and celebrated by the Jewish people today. It can for all of us just be a good biblical story or a reality of the power of our LORD and HIS faithfulness of watching over HIS word to perform it. If we can believe that incredible story why can we not trust HIM for every detail of our life and relinquish our control and truly let HIM be LORD?

As we know, Moses under instructions from the LORD stretched out his hand over the sea and the LORD drove the sea back and turned it into dry ground. The Israelites crossed over the dry ground although there was water on the left and right side with the Egyptians pursuing them until the LORD again told Moses to stretch out his hand over the sea with the result of the sea going back to its original place and the LORD sweeping the Egyptians into the sea where none of them survived.

When we are facing our Red Sea, may we remember that nothing is impossible for HIM and "We do not need to be Afraid."

MOSES (Transformation)

Moses said to the people, "Do not be Afraid. GOD has come to test you, so that the fear of GOD will be with you to keep you from sinning."
Exodus 20:20

When the LORD is trying to communicate to us, HE certainly knows how to set a table and lay things out. We have Moses on Mt Sinai receiving the Ten Commandments and then HE gets the Israelites attention with thunder and lightning as well as the mountain in smoke and hearing the trumpet. Typical of many we want GOD, but without even realizing it we want HIM at a distance. If HE gets too close something within us might be revealed that we do not want revealed. In fact, they stayed at a distance and advised Moses to "speak to us yourself and we will listen. But do not have GOD speak to us or we will die." (Exodus 20:19) Isn't it so sad that we do not lay everything about us open to the LORD even though there is nothing hidden from HIM and yet we wonder why we never hear from the LORD or experience HIS fullness and faithfulness.

Moses of course is having revelations of the holiness of our GOD and his words are meant for not only the Israelites but are appropriate for us as well. When GOD tests us HE knows what is in our heart, but the testing process reveals to us what we need to know about what is in our own heart as well.

In this particular scripture the Israelites needed the fear of GOD to keep them from sinning. If they had the fear of GOD, they wouldn't sin. There is a major difference between being Afraid of the LORD and fearing the LORD. Being Afraid of GOD is simply to have a distorted perspective of GOD and not being able to trust HIM. Fearing the LORD is to have a healthy reverence of HIM and HIS holiness. I would hope that in these days before the return of the LORD our love for HIM is simply that we love HIM above everything else. When Moses is telling the Israelites "Do not be Afraid" he is trying to tell them that they are entering into something beautiful which is a process of fearing the LORD and out of that love process they will love HIM above everything and everyone else.

Let's be encouraged as we examine the transformation of Moses as the LORD is threatening to destroy the Israelites who had become corrupt while Moses was receiving the tablets on the Mountain. In fact, Moses in Exodus 32:11-13, quotes back to the LORD the Covenant, which in part was the same scripture that GOD used to identify HIMSELF to Moses at the burning bush. We see in Exodus 32:14 the LORD relented and did not bring on HIS people the disaster HE had threatened. This principle is a key in our testing time as well. When the LORD gives you a word, in many cases it will be quite some time before the promise comes about, but in our testing and with reverence, we can remind the LORD of HIS promise. What it signifies to the LORD is that we trust HIS word to us, and we are standing and believing in HIM to fulfill HIS word.

Remember that previously Moses hid his face from GOD, and now in Exodus 33:12-23 we see Moses identifying that it is the LORD'S presence that distinguishes the LORD'S people from all the other people on the earth. That is such a powerful statement for us today and helps us to understand how set apart we really are because of HIS presence. I love the conversation between Moses and the LORD. To highlight just two verses, Then Moses said, "Now show me your glory". (*Verse 18*) and "But, HE said, "You cannot see MY face, for no one may see ME and live". This is the same Moses in Exodus 3:6 who was Afraid to look at GOD. That is personal transformation that comes out of intimacy with the LORD. Can we be honest with HIM and acknowledge that deep, deep down in our being there are things that hold us back from true intimacy with HIM, but we desire to have HIM heal those things that bind us. Like Moses can we be transformed and desire to truly see HIM. Let us remember that Moses initially hid his face because he was Afraid to look at GOD. "Don't be Afraid" so HE can reveal HIMSELF to you but fear the holiness of our LORD when HE is testing you because HE is keeping you from sinning.

JOSHUA & CALEB

If the LORD is pleased with us, HE will lead us into that land, a land flowing with milk and honey, and will give it to us. Only do not rebel against the LORD. And Do not be Afraid of the people of the land, because we will swallow them up. Their protection is gone, but the LORD is with us. Do not be Afraid of them"
Numbers 14:8, 9

This scripture was very significant for this generation of Israelites but also in our present days it is critical for us as well. We are to learn from what happened and why it happened so that we can apply it to our own walk with the LORD. Please join me from two different perspectives.

1. The Israelites were dealing with crossing the Jordan to not only enter the Promised Land but just as significantly they were crossing into the Promised Land to possess the land as an inheritance from the LORD. In these last days many of us have received

an insight into GOD'S purposes for our lives and we are waiting to cross our Jordan and about to enter into the promises and purposes we believe GOD has for us.

2. The Israelites subsequently were looking at the giants and were afraid of them and as a result a generation of Israelites excluding Joshua and Caleb did not enter the Promised Land.

We in the western developed nations are equally afraid of being too radical in our love and submission to the LORDSHIP of JESUS CHRIST and have inadvertently kept ourselves from processing the perceived promises HE has given us. Their fear bound their faith and our fear can bind our faith. A number of years ago during my devotion I was trying to manipulate the LORD into letting HIM know I was ready for HIM to really use me for HIS Kingdom. When it was obvious to me, HE was not biting I dropped the subject but later was pondering the matter and I casually asked the LORD "How long does it take to be prepared for

YOU to really use us?" and HE spoke these words "It depends on the price one is prepared to pay." The SPIRIT of GOD fell upon me and I started weeping, and the following words came out of me from the unction of the HOLY SPIRIT "Yes and they walked in the desert for 40 years and still never crossed into the Promised Land".

As we know 12 spies went into the Promised Land and 10 came back with a negative report, yet Joshua and Caleb came back with faith and a good report. Moses is trying to encourage the Israelites and he focuses on 4 themes:

1. If the LORD is pleased with us HE will lead us.
2. Do not rebel against the LORD.
3. Do not be afraid of the people of the Land for we know our battle is not against flesh and blood.
4. The LORD is with us and for Joshua and Caleb that was the key.

Is it possible that when GOD is really in full control of us then we are not walking in fear? That is the root issue even though HIS vision and purpose for us is so much more than we could ever imagine or dream.

In the case of the Israelites the LORD was giving them their own land and yet they refused to believe in HIM and walk in faith. It is important for us to understand how significant it was with the LORD. The ten spies who came back and spread the bad report were struck down and died of a plague before the LORD. Everyone twenty years and older did not enter the promised land and their children were shepherds for forty years – one year for each of the forty days the spies explored the land before they crossed into the Promised Land. The exception; Caleb and Joshua and the LORD'S reason is given.

"Not one of you will enter the land I swore with uplifted hand to make your home, except Caleb son of Jephunneh and Joshua son of Nun. Numbers 14:30 and in Deuteronomy the LORD gives the key to Caleb and Joshua is because they followed HIM "wholeheartedly"

Just because the LORD gives us a vision or dream does not mean it will automatically come to pass. HE waited a full generation to finally bring HIS children into the Promised Land, however if we do not follow Him "wholeheartedly" we too may miss our destiny. If we are seriously following the LORD there will always be giants, walls and deceptions that the enemy wants to place before us, but the key is to trust HIM and "Do not be afraid "– go for it.

MOSES (Mentoring)

Do not show partiality in judging; hear both small and great alike. Do not be Afraid of any man, for judgement belongs to GOD. Bring me any case too hard for you, and I will hear it.
Deuteronomy 1:17

Moses was clearly carrying too heavy a burden alone and realizes that he can not bear the burdens, problems and disputes of the people, so eventually there were chosen from each tribe some wise, understanding and respected men and set over the people. I love Moses' heart and his counsel to his appointed leaders which should serve us as leaders today as well, but let's take a quick look at what the Apostle Paul gave as the blueprint for the New Testament church of today in 1Corintihians 12:27-31: Now you are the Body of CHRIST, and each one of you is a part of it. And in the church GOD has appointed first of all apostles, second prophets, third teachers, then workers of miracles, also those having gifts of healing, those able to help others, those with gifts of administration, and those speaking in different kinds of tongues. Are all apostles? Are all prophets? Are all teachers? Do all work miracles? Do all have gifts of healing? Do all speak in tongues? Do all interpret? But eagerly desire the greater gifts.

We see great wisdom from Moses that aids leaders today in being free to deal with all people, which of course is not to show partiality in judging as well as hearing both small and great alike. It is very easy and human to spend the extra time with those whom we are close to or we feel have much to offer. Moses then gets into the key principle "Do not be Afraid of any man."

When placed in positions of spiritual leadership or authority, we must have the fundamentals of character, integrity and our relationship with others such as: that as servants we are to serve, think more highly of others than ourselves, etc, however, we should also be carrying an anointing from the HOLY SPIRIT that only comes from HIM specifically for the appointing and gifting HE has given us.   Unfortunately, there are many in the service of the LORD today who were not called into their present positions and have been wrongfully selected by man and not by the LORD.

Moses helps us as we cannot help serve others if we are Afraid to ask the tough questions and Afraid to speak the truth. We love to be loved. We love to be well thought of.   We love to show our compassion, our insight, our wisdom, etc. but Moses, who knows something about leadership says, "Do not be Afraid of man".   The story of Moses has much to teach us and the testimony about Moses is clearly stated in Deuteronomy 34: 10-12 Since then, no prophet has risen in Israel like Moses, whom the LORD knew face to face, who did all those miraculous signs and wonders the LORD sent him to do in Egypt-to Pharaoh and to all his officials and to his whole land. For no one has ever shown the mighty power or performed the awesome deeds that Moses did in the sight of Israel.

What a tribute to the person of Moses. As always when we read and study our biblical heroes we need to see if anything applies to us that we can learn form them or what they experienced. I believe that what Moses stated about "Afraid of man" it is not the physical fear of our well being but helps us to also better understand why we are so reluctant or hesitant to share the Gospel of JESUS CHRIST. If we are bold in our faith we are going to be looked at by different people at different times as being really "odd", really "strange", really "religious" and of course it all has an affect on our self image. What would our employer, customer, school teacher, neighbour, fellow worker or social acquaintances think of us? Sadly, the enemy deceives us and we back off when we should be going forward with the Good news. I am not talking about not waiting for the leading of the SPIRIT but let's make sure that is not an excuse. As the Apostle Paul states "Woe to me if I do not preach the Gospel". Sometimes it is the littlest word that can have an eternal change in a person's life. I recall listening to a former National Hockey league player give his testimony and of all things the one little seed that was planted in his life came from a very young boy who along with many other children waiting at an arena to get an autograph yelled out to the professional player who by his own confession was full of himself at the time "Hey—--if you died today where would you go? Heaven or hell? The hockey player stated that he had never thought of that question and it stayed with him. What opportunities has the LORD given us that we have backed off from because of fear of compromising ourselves?

Spiritual leadership can be dealing with our children, our co-workers, neighbours, spouses, family members, bible study group, social or business groups. We are servants of the most high and HE is jealous of our love. How can we love HIM unconditionally, truly serve HIM and yet be conscious of man and what he might think? Moses offers to hear the hard cases but all of us in leadership must at all times remember we have the HOLY SPIRIT as our COUNSELOR, and HE desires us to go to HIM. Receive from HIM because HE alone has the appropriate wisdom. Remember "Don't be afraid."

JOSHUA

"Have I not commanded you? Be strong and courageous. Do not be Terrified; do not be discouraged, for the LORD your GOD will be with you wherever you go."

Joshua 1:9

Can you imagine being addressed by GOD HIMSELF and as HE is wrapping up HIS instructions, HE repeats some points that we have noted in this scripture? Joshua has been given the task of not only leading the Hebrews into the Promised Land but possessing the land that was promised initially to Abraham, Isaac and Jacob who had never possessed the land. We know the challenge of Moses in leading these people but Joshua who has now received the instructions from the LORD has some strong points on his side.

1. Moses has mentored Joshua and although much has been talked about and written regarding mentoring, the one key component that Joshua observed and

learned from Moses was entering into the presence of our GOD. That was fundamental to Moses and should be to those of us who mentor as well. What is being observed about the presence of GOD? (*Exodus 33:15*) The presence of GOD is the key to us and to those we mentor.

2. Joshua was filled with the SPIRIT of wisdom because Moses had laid his hands on him. You can't pass on something you don't have. (*Deuteronomy 34:12*)

3. Joshua was commissioned by the LORD (*Deuteronomy 31:14*). How sad it is to see so many being commissioned by everyone but the LORD.

4. The LORD will be with Joshua wherever he goes, and HE has given the same promise to us. HE will never leave us nor forsake us because in the New Covenant HE lives within us.

Joshua needed to be strong and courageous to be really used of the LORD, and so do we. We then see the counsel of the LORD to Joshua "Do not be Terrified" and do not be discouraged". Anybody who is really making a difference will testify that there are some days that you wonder what it is all about. As we will see later with Joshua, that is the maturing process of spiritual leadership. In Joshua's case, the Israelites successfully crossed the Jordan River, had their circumcision at Gilgal receiving a most unique and unusual military victory at Jericho where they walked in obedience to the LORD. Then they encounter sin in the camp of Joshua. We see that many times when we experience victory the "feeling good attitude" can begin to affect our judgement and the result is sin and trouble with GOD and the enemy. As we see in the battle at Ai, after Joshua and all Israel dealt with Achan and his sin issue, ultimately stoning him to death, the LORD again began speaking to Joshua.

Then the LORD said to Joshua, "Do not be Afraid; do not be discouraged. Take the whole army with you and go up and attack Ai. For I have delivered into your hands the king of Ai, his people, his city and his land." (*Joshua 8:1*)

The LORD in His grace understands more than we do the affect of being Afraid and discouraged. When we are moving in the things of the LORD and issues such as sin, assumption, etc arise that causes us to stumble it is quite normal for us to back off, become apprehensive, disappointed and discouraged.

We see the faithfulness of our LORD and HIS encouragement and motivation for Joshua BEFORE HE gives Joshua the assurance of strategy and victory in Ai. Again, before Joshua goes to Gideon for battle the LORD encourages him. The LORD says to Joshua "Do not be Afraid of them; I have given them into your hand. Not one of them will be able to withstand you." (*Joshua 10:8*). It is pretty obvious there is a clean, consistent message from the LORD for Joshua. In the battle against the 5 Amorite Kings, the LORD hurled large hailstones down from the sky killing more enemies than were killed by the whole of the Israelites. As mentioned earlier, the maturing process of Joshua comes into play and guess what Joshua is now saying to the Israelites. Joshua said to them "Do not be Afraid; do not be discouraged. Be strong and courageous. This is what the LORD will do to all the enemies you are going to fight." (*Joshua 10:25*)

Joshua has got it! Where have we seen this before? Isn't it beautiful to see the processing and preparation of Joshua so that what was imparted into Joshua by the LORD resonated in Joshua as he saw the faithfulness and trustworthiness of the LORD, so that his words were from a reality foundation. Joshua was not a robot. What the LORD initially spoke to Joshua was then supported by the acts of GOD so that faith in the Faithful ONE was built into Joshua to the point that he could echo the LORD'S words to the Israelites so that their faith in the Faithful ONE would also be realized.

When we speak the LORD'S word on behalf of GOD, HE always confirms HIS word as we see in Joshua 11:6 where Joshua and the Israelites were going to war against the Northern Kings. The LORD said to Joshua, "Do not be Afraid of them, because by this time tomorrow I will hand all of them over to Israel, slain. You are to hamstring their horses and burn their chariots." If we placed ourselves in the Israelites shoes, can you imagine the level of faith we would have in the LORD and our confidence in our leader Joshua, who had been commissioned by the LORD to lead us?

The question we need to ask ourselves is where is our belief system and how tested and real is it because as we can see we can't lead others where we have not walked? The LORD was not just leading HIS people into the Promised Land, but HE was leading HIS people into the Promised Land to possess it, and there is a major difference. Today, the LORD, JESUS CHRIST desires that we possess and own our own destiny in HIM, and it just doesn't automatically happen.

As Joshua and the Israelites had to go to war to possess the land so must we and let us not be naïve but realize there is a price to pay when we go to war. Our war is not against flesh and blood but against the powers and principalities of darkness, but when we go to war, we go in the name of JESUS CHRIST, washed in HIS blood, serving HIM and HIS Kingdom. We can not operate and serve HIM in Fear but in Faith knowing we can totally and unconditionally trust HIM. As our reality of trust matures, we too will be able to state as Joshua was able to claim, "Do not be afraid."

GIDEON

With the tip of the staff that was in his hand, the angel of the LORD touched the meat and the unleavened bread. Fire flared from the rock, consuming the meat and the bread. And the angel of the LORD disappeared. When Gideon realized that it was the angel of the LORD, he exclaimed, "Ah, SOVEREIGN LORD! I have seen the angel of the LORD face to face!"

But the LORD said to him, "Peace! Do not be Afraid. You are not going to die."

Judges 6:21-23

If there is one person most of us can identify with, it probably is Gideon. How many times do we say to the HOLY SPIRIT "If this is YOU speaking please give me a sign"? Or "I believe this is what YOU are telling me to do but I need a confirmation." "HOLY SPIRIT if this is YOU leading me to do this then I need a confirmation ". Many of us like Gideon are just as overwhelmed when we have a major spiritual encounter. It is important to get confirmation of what you feel the LORD is telling you.

To give the setting the proper backdrop, the Israelites did evil in the eyes of the LORD and for seven years HE gave them into the hands of the Midianites (*Judges 6:1*) and the Israelites cried out to the LORD. An angel of the LORD came to Gideon and among other statements called Gideon a "mighty warrior" but Gideon thought it best to advise the LORD that the clan Gideon came from was the weakest and that Gideon was the least in the family. What is your excuse(s) when the HOLY SPIRIT begins to try and get your attention, or do you inform the LORD that HE has made a mistake in choosing you?

The scripture that comes to mind when you have such a setting is: But GOD chose the foolish things of the world to shame the wise; GOD chose the weak things of the world to shame the strong (*I Corinthians 1:27*). Did GOD make a mistake, or did HE see Gideon transformed into a mighty warrior? What does HE see in us if we submit to HIM and

HIS transforming work in our lives? Is HE truly the potter (transformer) in our daily life and are we the clay allowing HIM to mould us and change us into what HE created us to be?

Isn't it beautiful to see the comfort and reassurance the LORD gave Gideon and yet does not release him from his tasks? As we encounter the HOLY SPIRIT in a special way it is just as beautiful when HE fills us with Supernatural peace and gives us the comfort and reassurance that HE knows what we need. On one hand HE is calling Gideon a mighty warrior and on the other HE is saying "Don't be Afraid".

I love and am encouraged by the progress of Gideon and to Gideon's credit he moves forward with the LORD and does what the LORD asks of him:

1. Tear down your father's altar to Baal.
2. Cut down the Asherah pole beside it.
3. Build a proper altar to the LORD.

Before we go to war, we need by the guidance of the HOLY SPIRIT to yield to the things that the LORD knows need to be put right. We are very good at putting the things right as we see them because that keeps us in control, but we need to allow HIM to put things right as HE sees them because HE then is in control. Control issues are in reality LORDSHIP issues. Gideon obeys the LORD and now he is ready for war with the Midianites after one more confirmation (fleece). How can we not love our GOD with passion and faith when we see what HE does? HE agrees to give Gideon one more fleece, which of course would build up Gideon's faith and confidence. Then HE turns around and tells Gideon he has too many men in his camp, so the men who tremble with fear are excused from the battle and 22,000 leave and 10,000 remain. The LORD sifts through the 10,000 and there are now 300 ready for battle. There is only one who is to receive glory for this battle and that is our GOD. It is the same for everything we do. We need to always remember who gets the glory and that it truly is our mighty LORD. Gideon asked the LORD for a fleece which the LORD allowed when Gideon had 22,000 and now, he has 300! The intimacy and wisdom of GOD shines through and HE says to Gideon at night before the battle "If you are Afraid to attack, go down to the camp with your servant Purah and listen to what they are saying. Afterward, you will be encouraged to attack the camp." So Gideon and Purah, his servant went down to the outpost of the camp. (*Judges 7:10, 11*)

GOD in HIS great purposes didn't at this point say to Gideon "Don't be Afraid to attack" but "if you are Afraid to attack" and gave Gideon a strategy that would encourage Gideon to attack. That strategy was for Gideon to overhear a dream and the interpretation of the dream between two of their enemies that GOD was going to give the Midianites and the whole camp into Gideon's hand. Gideon all of a sudden turns into two people:

1. A Worshipper. After overhearing the dream and its interpretation he worships GOD. Are you a real worshipper of the LORD?

2. A Mighty Warrior. A mighty warrior will say things like "Get Up" "Watch me" "Follow my lead" which are the words Gideon spoke to his men as they went to conquer the Midianites. Have you allowed the LORD to transform you into a Mighty Warrior?

We must all be encouraged from our LORD to go deeper and higher in HIM and to fulfill HIS purpose for our lives. Just "Don't be Afraid."

ELIJAH AND THE WIDOW

Elijah said to her, "Don't be Afraid. Go home and do as you have said. But first make a small cake bread for me from what you have and bring it to me, and then make something for yourself and your son. For this is what the LORD, the GOD of Israel, says: 'The jar of flour will not be used up and the jug of oil will not run dry until the day the LORD gives rain on the land".
1 Kings 17:13-14

The prophet Elijah whose name means "The LORD is my GOD" was sent by the LORD to oppose both Baal worship and those leaders engaged in it specifically King Ahab and as we are introduced to Elijah we find him speaking on behalf of the LORD to Ahab stating that there will be neither dew or rain in the next few years until at Elijah's word. Wow, what a statement to be made but Elijah had been prepared by the LORD and spoke the LORD'S word. After giving this word to Ahab the LORD instructed Elijah to go to the Kerith Ravine where the LORD would take care of all his needs.

Some time later the LORD directs Elijah to a widow at the town gate in Zarephath who is on her way home to prepare a final meal for herself and her son, as there is no food left except for their final meal. She has a handful of flour in a jar and a little oil in another jar. The widow appears to have resigned herself to the fact that her son and her are about to die from starvation during a drought time on the land.

Elijah came to Zarephath under instruction from the LORD for two reasons:

1. He has been at the Kerith Ravine where the LORD ordered the ravens to feed him daily and where he had been drinking water from the brook before it dried up.

2. The LORD told Elijah that HE had commanded a widow to supply Elijah with food.

Why did Elijah tell the widow not to be Afraid? To confirm to her that she and her son were not going to die? Or- that the prophetic words Elijah spoke to her were from the LORD and would be true? Or - that she was by faith to put Elijah's feeding before she fed herself and her son even though there might not be enough left over for them?

Is it reasonable to assume that each and every one of the points above could be true by themselves or collectively? What we do know is that the LORD told Elijah that HE had commanded a widow to supply Elijah with food. Scripture does not detail how the LORD commanded the widow. It also appears that the widow had resigned herself to the fact that she and her son were going to die shortly. Put ourselves in the widow's place and look at the meagre amount of oil and flour and then all of a sudden Elijah tells us that the oil and flour jugs will not dry up from continually producing oil and flour during the water drought in the land.

Is this Elijah a nut case trying to manipulate a last meal for himself or is he a prophetic man of GOD who had the mind and word of GOD and in obedience to the LORD speaks the word.?

So where does Elijah come up with this extra verbiage he gives to the widow, which in fact proves to be totally accurate? In this particular case scripture does not reveal the exchange of the specific word of the LORD given to Elijah and subsequently the widow but clearly Elijah had the right word of the LORD. What we do know is the ultimate truth of the word given by Elijah to the widow was found to be accurate. A word of the LORD will always be true. Unfortunately, on one hand we have an abuse of the prophetic which is in fact not from the LORD and on the other hand we have many in the body who believe the word of the LORD was only given to the Old Testament prophets. Without going into a teaching seminar on operating prophetically, let me share some personal observations about the prophetic. First of all, to the naysayers, let me agree that there can be an abuse of the prophetic and some prophetic words are so general you could drive a truck through them. Having stated that, you can choose to park yourself where you are but you are missing something of GOD from GOD. We need to remember the LORD'S word always lines up with scripture.

I believe the HOLY SPIRIT utilizes two different means to communicate prophetically to a group or an individual. All true prophecy comes ONLY from the HOLY SPIRIT operating through people HE chooses by:

1. Hearing the voice of the HOLY SPIRIT and communicating that message from GOD as a spokesperson sent from GOD.

2. A seer is one who receives visions, dreams or pictures and shares what they have seen; such as Daniel, Elisha, Zechariah, etc. In this scripture, "Do not be Afraid' would help prepare the widow to accept the word of the LORD that she and her son would not only have enough left over after feeding Elijah but they would receive a supernatural daily provision of oil and flour in their empty jars. Death and daily food is no longer an issue compliments of a loving and faithful GOD

who loves to love and provide in ways that only HE can do.

When our LORD gives you a word, receive it and be prepared as Elijah was to speak it out to whomever our LORD directs you. Be encouraged "Follow the way of love and eagerly desire spiritual gifts, especially the gift of prophecy" (*1 Corinthians 14:1*). We see in this example GOD'S love and prophecy working together as HE reveals it to HIS prophet Elijah who in obedience speaks it to a widow who assumes she and her son are about to die. "Don't be Afraid."

ELIJAH

The angel of the LORD said to Elijah, "Go down with him; Do not be Afraid of him." So Elijah got up and went down with him to the king.

2 Kings 1:15

Elijah had experienced the highs and lows of being the LORD'S representative fully aware that King Ahab's wife, Jezebel had been killing off the LORD'S prophets and Elijah challenged Ahab to bring the prophets of Baal and Asherah including the people of Israel to the top of Mt. Carmel to determine which God would answer by bringing down fire on the altar. As we know the one and only LORD, GOD ALMIGHTY brought down the fire and the people recognized the LORD as GOD. Elijah had the false prophets brought to the Kishon Valley and had them slaughtered. Jezebel heard of what had taken place and determined to have Elijah killed and Elijah was Afraid for his life and ran and eventually the LORD met with him and restored him.

Subsequently after King Ahab had died, Elijah, the prophet, had given the word of the LORD to the messengers of the King of Samaria advising them that the king would not leave the bed he was laying on as he was going to die because the king had consulted a pagan god instead of the GOD of Israel.

Let's agree that is a pretty clear message that GOD had Elijah give the kings messenger considering that the LORD had to direct Elijah where to locate the messengers to give them the unsolicited message.

The Kings reaction in 2 Kings 1:9-13: He sent his captain with fifty men on three occasions to Elijah who was sitting on top of a hill.

The captain's first two messages to Elijah: "Man of GOD, the king says, 'Come down!' "

Elijah's response to the first two captain's requests: "If I am a man of GOD, may fire come down from heaven and consume you and your fifty men!"   In baseball terms, we could say "two up and two strikeouts", or in spiritual terms, "Elijah was clearly a man of GOD, speaking as a messenger of GOD to the King of a Nation with a serious message from GOD."

The third visit: The third captain, along with 50 men approached Elijah still on the top of the hill but this time the captain addressed this man of GOD, begging for his life and the lives of his 50 men. We have to at least give the third captain credit for knowing who he was dealing with.

GOD'S directive: "Go down with him, Do not be Afraid of him." (2Kings 1:15)

Afraid of whom? Clearly the LORD was referring to the King of Samaria.

Going to the King: Elijah went with the captain and his fifty men and confirmed the word of the LORD to the king.

Conclusion: The king died as per the word of the LORD given by the prophet Elijah.

Summary: Our LORD is very strategic in all that HE does and says when HIS servants walk in obedience to HIM.
The GOD of Israel was grieved that HE was not acknowledged, and HE was determined to reveal HIMSELF as the GOD of Israel. HE chose to deal directly and personally with the King of Samaria by giving him a strong word through HIS prophet, Elijah and by exhibiting HIS fire and power to not only the king but also those close to the king and thus the nation. By utilizing HIS prophet Elijah in HIS acts of fire and power, it caused the king's third captain to acknowledge that the man of GOD (Elijah) took his instructions from the GOD of Israel and not the King of Samaria. Because the LORD was dealing with the king and indirectly the nation, HE spoke to Elijah with the words of comfort and courage, "Do not be Afraid of him." You would think that after successfully confronting the first two captains and watching what happened to them, that Elijah would have no concerns about climbing down

the hill and going with this captain who clearly understood Elijah's authority. This captain obviously feared this man of GOD, but Elijah knew that the fire and power was not of him but of his GOD. The LORD knew that Elijah needed the comfort of HIS words and spoke them to him. This enabled Elijah to accomplish the task of giving GOD'S word to the King of Samaria. Interestingly when you examine all the events of Elijah's life in speaking and acting on behalf of the LORD you would wonder why the LORD would need to tell Elijah "Do not be Afraid" before he spoke to the king of Samaria, but our loving and faithful LORD knows and understands our needs on behalf of the LORD'S work. Remember if GOD gives you a task, "Don't be Afraid."

ELISHA

When the servant of the man of GOD got up and went out early the next morning, an army with horses and chariots had surrounded the city. "Oh my LORD, what shall we do?" the servant asked.

"Don't be Afraid," the prophet answered. "Those who are with us are more than those who are with them."

And Elisha prayed, "O LORD, open his eyes so he may see." Then the LORD opened the servant's eyes, and he looked and saw the hills full of horses and chariots of fire all around Elisha.
2 Kings 6:15-17

Elisha was called by the LORD when HIS prophet Elijah found Elisha plowing the fields with oxen at the family farm. Elijah threw his cloak around Elisha and that act would confirm the way of the LORD'S calling and commissioning for Elisha. Elisha was Elijah's attendant and he was like Elijah's shadow. When the LORD was about to take Elijah to heaven in a whirlwind and Elisha would not leave his side, they have this beautiful exchange that shows us the heart and spiritual understanding of Elisha in

2 Kings: 2-9 When they had crossed, Elijah said to Elisha, "Tell me, what can I do for you before I am taken from you?" "Let me inherit a double portion of your spirit," Elisha replied.

At this time, the king of Aram was at war with Israel and the man of GOD. Elisha, the prophet of GOD had kept the king of Israel informed of strategic moves by the king of Aram to the point that one of the officers of the king of Aram advised the king "but Elisha, the prophet who is in Israel, tells the king of Israel the very words you speak in your bedroom." (2 Kings 6:12) Talk about a unique intelligence officer who clearly was not using electronic devices but had intimate foreknowledge of everything the king of Aram spoke in his bedroom because of the ways of our LORD and the intimacy that Elisha had with the LORD.

We can read about this intimacy between Elisha and the LORD as a history story but as we move closer to the return of the LORD, there will be a need for us to walk in such intimacy. The desire however, for us today as followers of JESUS CHRIST is to walk in total intimacy with the LORD who calls us to love HIM with all our heart, mind and being. It is out of that intimacy with our LORD that revelation comes. HE is the same yesterday, today and forever.

Elisha became a target of the king of Aram who sent a strong force with horses and chariots to capture Elisha and one of Elisha's aides gets up and sees the city surrounded and of course panics.

Elisha tries to settle down his aide "Don't be Afraid" and then takes his aide and us into the supernatural because this man of GOD knows the hosts of Heaven are far stronger than the Aramean forces sent to capture him. Do we have the insight of Elisha or better yet, do we really believe and if not, let Elisha's prayer be our personal prayer so that the LORD would give us eyes to see the hosts of Heaven? "Dear LORD, open our eyes so we may see."

The LORD opened Elisha's servant's eyes so he could see the heavenly hosts, the hills full of horses and chariots of fire all around Elisha and may we desire to have our eyes open as well. There is a natural world and a supernatural world, and may we desire to have revelation as HE gives us grace to see. We are much more comfortable being in the natural, but we should desire to have HIM allow us to see and serve HIM in the supernatural as well. Please allow me to pray from Ephesians 1:17-19 for you. "I keep asking that the GOD of our LORD JESUS CHRIST, the glorious FATHER, may give you the SPIRIT of wisdom and revelation, so that you may know HIM better. I pray also that the eyes of your heart may be enlightened in order that you may know the hope to which HE has called you, the riches of HIS glorious inheritance in the saints, and HIS incomparably great power for us who believe." Amen.

It is important to realize that when our eyes are supernaturally opened, we will see things that are in the SPIRIT and we need to remember, "Do not be Afraid."

ISAIAH - HEZAKIAH

When King Hezekiah's officials came to Isaiah, Isaiah said to them, "Tell your master, 'This is what the LORD says: Do not be Afraid of what you have heard – those words with which the underlings of the king of Assyria have blasphemed ME. Listen! I am going to put such a spirit in him that when he hears a certain report, he will return to his own country, and there I will have him cut down with the sword.' " 2 Kings19: 5-7

Isaiah, son of Amoz spent most of his life in Jerusalem while King Hezekiah was serving and wrote during the period marking the expansion of the Assyrian empire and the decline of Israel. Isaiah's name means "the LORD saves" and we see in the book of Isaiah not only the full extent of GOD'S judgement but also HIS salvation.

In our day of instant communication, both the good and the bad; truth and deception, there has never been such a potential cultural manipulation by the media into what and how we hear or observe to control our thinking patterns. While many call the message 'the spin' the root of it is a "spirit". For example, if you ask believers about taking a trip or a tour of Israel, they will tell you that they would love to go for a visit to the Holy Land on one hand and on the other how unsafe it is even though they have never gone. The reality is that unless there is a time of war or unusual circumstance using basic safety travel skills that you would normally do when you visit any city in North America you may go and enjoy a safe trip. Why then the fear? It is reported through the media with subtle backdrop pictures, with subtle wording and we draw our own conclusions that it is not safe. The media does not tell us NOT to go but we draw our own conclusion from what is reported, and we miss one of the most important trips for a Christian to take.

What the LORD, through the prophet Isaiah, is telling King Hezekiah's officials is "Don't be Afraid of what you have learned" – and then the prophet continues on with the word from the LORD.

We need to have real discernment from the LORD of what we hear and from who, whether it be rumours, gossip, negativity, exaggerations, manipulation or control.

In this particular case, the words that King Hezekiah heard were in fact a blasphemy and challenge against the living LORD and thus fear and intimidation against the people, but the LORD speaks through Isaiah and states how HE is going to deal with the king of Assyria and true to HIS word HE does deal with the king of Assyria.

What I find so neat is that the LORD is sharing through Isaiah with King Hezekiah as HE would a friend. All that the LORD needed to share with King Hezekiah is to "Not be Afraid" of what he had heard but the reality is that HE brings King Hezekiah and thus ourselves into this whole matter of how the king of Assyria was challenging HIS reality of being the living GOD and how HE was going to deal with the king of Assyria because of the king's blasphemy against HIM. We must also remember that HE truly is the living CHRIST, to be honoured and revered but HE also desires to share with us HIS beautiful personal insights as we would with a true friend. We can hear HIM, but if we hear something from the father of lies that is contrary to the word we need to "Not be Afraid."

I believe too often we limit our GOD because we do not know how awesome HE really is and as a result, we don't know or have not experienced HIS ways and thus have a lack of faith to really follow HIM. As we saw with King Hezekiah, he sought and consulted with Isaiah the prophet, however let us examine how King Jehosaphat dealt with the report that armies were coming against him and his people in 2 Chronicles 20. First of all, the king resolved to inquire of the LORD and proclaimed a fast. May I challenge you and ask you when you resolved to inquire enough to fast? On a personal note, I remember the first time I fasted which took place on my first Easter as a born again believer and follower of JESUS CHRIST. Please understand I love my food; however, I just wanted to honour the LORD and decided to fast for 24 hours. At about the 23 hour and 59th minute I had my hand on the fridge door waiting and counting the last minute and out of nowhere, the HOLY SPIRIT whispered "John, I would like you to fast to the 40th hour." I had mixed emotions as I was obviously both thrilled and startled to unexpectedly hear the voice of GOD and yet the battle of my flesh cried out for comfort. In the next 16 hours, my LORD took me past my flesh into incredible intimacy with HIM and on the 40th hour HE gave me revelation of destiny that changed my life. Years later when I was doing my first 40 day fast, I remembered and chuckled at my first time of fasting for 40 hours and how the LORD had honoured it.

 In any case, we see where the King "resolved" and called for a fast and during this time the word says, "Then the SPIRIT of the LORD came upon Jahaziel" who said to King Jehoshaphat "This is what the LORD says to you "Do not be Afraid or discouraged because of this vast army. For the battle is not yours, but GOD'S", and again later on "Do not be Afraid; do not be discouraged. Go out to face them tomorrow, and the LORD will be with you"', and all the people fell down in worship before the LORD. That is worship and it seems to set a foundation because the next morning worshippers went out in front of their army singing and praising the LORD and their enemies started fighting and destroying each other. As we can see from both examples GOD gave total victories in far different ways but both Kings wanted GOD'S attention.

As Kings and Priests, may we allow the HOLY SPIRIT to challenge us to have such a deep desire to hear from HIM on how to reach with HIS message those HE has placed in our lives for HIS eternal purposes. We might not consider ourselves a prophet like Isaiah or Jeremiah, but we are a servant of the LORD and we need to be a willing and open vessel to be used of the LORD. We might not give a word from the LORD to a King or Head of State, but it can be a neighbour, relative, co-worker, classmate or friend but let us also remember and take to heart the words the LORD gave to both of these Kings or to whomever HE may choose to speak to through us. We must be both open and "Not be Afraid."

DAVID – THE TEMPLE

"All this," David said, "I have in writing from the hand of the LORD upon me, and HE gave me understanding in all the details of the plan."

David also said to Solomon his son, "Be strong and courageous, and do the work. Do not be Afraid or discouraged, for the LORD GOD, my GOD is with you. HE will not fail you or forsake you until all the work for the service of the temple of the LORD is finished.

I Chronicles 28:19, 20

King David summoned all the officials of Israel to gather in Jerusalem including his son, Solomon, where he shared his heart and personal journey. Although the LORD chose David, a man after HIS own heart, to be the King of Israel, HE would not allow David to build the Temple for the LORD because David was a warrior who had shed blood. We need to understand what David is initially introducing as he is addressing the officials and his son Solomon. I Chronicles 28: 2 King David rose to his feet and said: "Listen to me, my brothers and my people. I had it in my heart to build a house as a place of rest for the ark of the covenant of the LORD, for the footstool of our GOD, and I made plans to build it."

Three key points:

1. As we know the Ark of the Covenant meant the presence of the LORD and oh do we need to desire as David did to identify with our need of intimacy with the presence of our LORD.

2. The footstool that David is referring to is a place on earth where the LORD can rest HIS feet.

3. David was able to lay down HIS desires and plans for the LORD'S.

David's desire of course was to build the Temple and in fact David had received Temple plans in detail from the LORD. The LORD, however, chose David's son, Solomon and at this gathering David is instructing his officials with the LORD'S appointment of Solomon and is also addressing Solomon. Here we have David receiving the details for the Temple, but it was Solomon, his son, who was given the responsibility of building the temple and replaced his father as king of Israel.

What an incredible statement for David to be able to make that he had in writing from the hand of the LORD and the LORD gave David understanding in all details of the plan. That only comes from intimacy with the LORD.

Two clear points:

1. Let us desire such intimacy with the LORD that we too by the grace of our LORD can make such a statement.
2. That we, like David, will always acknowledge that is it the LORD who gives us understanding.

David is addressing the officials of Israel and Solomon towards the end of his life and at a period of transition where Solomon will become King of Israel and with the responsibility of building the temple and he is so much a hero of our faith. It is worth noting a few of the events that he accomplished with the LORD. David of course is the son of Jesse and ancestor of JESUS, killed Goliath, Musician to King Saul, anointed King by Samuel, a deep brotherly relationship with Jonathan even though Jonathan's father Saul wanted David dead, spared Saul's life, conquered Jerusalem, a mighty warrior, a psalmist, a prophet and of course along with other Psalms wrote the LORD is my shepherd in Psalm 23. Let's just agree David had the experiences both good and bad to mentor and counsel his son Solomon and the officials of Israel.

In David's comments to Solomon, you will note that being strong and courageous and working hard is not enough. In any major project there are peaks and valleys, but when we are involved in a Spiritual project, we are dealing with the powers and principalities of darkness and by the grace of GOD; we must not yield to the warfare. Of all the heroes of the faith, no one knew this more than David. David is talking from experience when he stated,

"Do not be Afraid or discouraged" because David speaks from a reality as a shepherd, king, psalmist, worshipper and mighty warrior.

David gives Solomon and us the keys:

1. The LORD GOD is with you.
2. HE will not fail you or forsake you.

Any project the LORD gives us, whether it is raising children, working in a difficult job, furthering our education or starting a Ministry, we know HE is with us. HE will not fail us, and HE will not forsake us. Just "Don't be Afraid or discouraged".

EZRA

Then the peoples around them set out to discourage the people of Judah and make them Afraid to go on building. They hired counselors to work against them and frustrate their plans during the entire reign of Cyrus king of Persia and down to the reign of Darius king of Persia.

Ezra 4:4-5

To help with the setting, the book of Ezra was during the time of the returning of the exiles and the re-building of the Temple and it was during the re-building that the opposition of the Temple was taking place.

As we see in scripture, the LORD consistently speaks either directly, through angels or HIS prophets, "Do not be Afraid," and several times we see the word "discouraged" also being part of the message. In most cases there is an insight into what we should not be Afraid of. However, unless we have walked in someone else's shoes it is easy for us to dismiss the matter as a part of history as it doesn't really impact us in a personal way.

In this particular scripture however, we see the people from Samaria attempting to discourage and make Afraid the exiles of Judah and Benjamin from rebuilding the temple for the LORD, the GOD of Israel. If the rebuilding program was for an office building or a home instead of the Temple for the LORD, would there be all of this effort to "discourage" and "make Afraid" the people? We also see the strategy and motivation being used to thwart the Temple for the LORD being completed. The hiring of counselors to work against the people and to frustrate their plans is a fairly serious effort of opposition and can be so subtle that we don't even realize that we or the project are under attack. Physical attack is something we all understand, but unfortunately a psychological attack is much easier disguised by the father of lies and thus, is not recognized by us as we normally have never been properly prepared on how to handle this warfare. So often when we talk of bullying or abusers we refer to physical abuse but the psychological abuse can and does cause such deep scars for life and is relevant in church circles today but it is not addressed in part as it does not leave the physical scars but it truly "comes from the pits of hell."

There are a couple of important principles we need better insight into:

1. Every time something doesn't go just right, does not mean it is from the enemy? It can be something the LORD is allowing to get our attention, or it can be something HE is using to change us. For example, if you are an impatient (selfish, prideful, judgemental, etc. etc.) person, it can be used by HIM to deal with these issues and we need to discern from the HOLY SPIRIT what the issues are.

2. The weapon of discouragement is a powerful tool in the hand of the enemy that he uses against the children of GOD. You must be honest with yourself and determine if you suffer from depression, stress, negativity, etc. as the enemy will always

attack at our greatest weaknesses. If you have these types of unresolved matters, it is important to bring them before our great COUNSELOR and COMFORTER to allow HIM to bring deliverance, healing and wholeness into our lives. We might find that the HOLY SPIRIT will in fact direct us to professional counseling as it is HIS desire to always help us walk in victory and be overcomers.

When we are truly submitted and serving HIM, under HIS LORDSHIP, we are in reality at war because we are in the Kingdom of GOD, serving our KING, who is advancing HIS Kingdom and there is opposition to HIM, HIS Kingdom and to those who our truly serving HIM. The greater the call, the greater the need for preparation and the bigger sacrifice we need to be prepared to pay. This example of warfare in scripture, I believe, is there for us so we can understand some of the plots of the enemy but do not operate in "being Afraid" since we are in HIM and HE has conquered all things including death itself.

NEHEMIAH

Therefore, I stationed some of the people behind the lowest points of the wall at the exposed places, posting them by families, with their swords, spears and bows. After I looked things over, I stood up and said to the nobles, the officials and the rest of the people, "Don't be Afraid of them. Remember the LORD, who is great and awesome, and fight for your brothers, your sons and your daughters, your wives and your homes."

When our enemies heard that we were aware of their plot and that GOD had frustrated it, we all returned to the wall, each to his own work.

Nehemiah 4:13,14,15

I just love the story of Nehemiah and believe there is so much that we can and need to learn from the heart of Nehemiah.

It is amazing how our LORD'S leaders have such a common thread in their spiritual make up, personality, and character development which all comes out of intimacy, surrender and brokenness. There is no short cut with our LORD. HIS resurrection power and authority comes to us, the New Testament Church, through the gift of the HOLY SPIRIT which JESUS CHRIST gave us at the Pentecost but the HOLY SPIRIT'S anointing power and authority comes out of brokenness. Nehemiah was a prepared vessel for our LORD to use. May we, like Nehemiah, be a prepared vessel. As we examine Nehemiah leading up to the addressing of his workers as they were rebuilding the wall in Jerusalem, I believe it is also appropriate for us to use this opportunity to examine ourselves as it helps us to know what our spiritual makeup is.

I feel this is a good time for you and me to allow the HOLY SPIRIT to reveal where we are today so we can be moved forward in HIM in the days ahead. Please join me in praying, "HOLY SPIRIT, as we examine Nehemiah, please reveal yourself to me and show me the areas of my life that YOU need to change. I wholeheartedly submit to YOU to make me a vessel YOU can really use. Amen"

Nehemiah learned that the Israelites who survived the exile are in great trouble and disgrace. The wall in Jerusalem is broken down and its gates have been burned with fire.

Nehemiah sat down and wept.

Q – When was the last time or have we ever been so grieved by similar circumstances that we needed to sit down and weep?

Q – What have we buried and not dealt with that we need to deal with? Or are we so indifferent that not much affects us?

Nehemiah mourned, fasted and then prayed.

Q – When was the last time that we fasted and prayed? Or have we ever? And if not, why not?

Nehemiah interceded for his people, confessing his and the people of Israel's sins.

Q – When was the last time or have we ever seriously interceded for people in your community or country? If not, why not?

Nehemiah literally asked for a leave of absence so that he could serve in rebuilding a city he did not live in.

Q – What would motivate us to take a leave of absence that was not self-serving?

Nehemiah's employer, King Artaxerxes gave Nehemiah his request and Nehemiah knew it was because the LORD'S hand was upon him.

Q – When we make our request, do we really know it was of the LORD?

Enemies in Jerusalem were disturbed that someone (Nehemiah) had come to promote the welfare of the Israelites.

Q – When we consider stepping into controversy it might be messy and there might be a personal price to pay. Would we really be prepared to pay the price?

Nehemiah had not told anyone what the LORD GOD put in his heart. It is good for us to remember that Nehemiah was first broken, wept, fasted and prayed and was an open vessel.

Q – What has GOD put in our heart to do? What did we do about it?

Nehemiah took leadership and risk of shame by sharing where and what the need was, and that GOD'S hand was upon him.

Q – Would we be that bold and speak with such authority?

When Nehemiah addressed the Israelites as the enemy's motives became clear, he knew as a leader rebuilding the walls and gates of Jerusalem, that the people needed to hear "Don't be Afraid" and "Remember the LORD."

Q – Has our faith in the Faithful ONE been so deep and mature that we could say with meaning and authority to others who are looking to us for leadership, "Don't be Afraid"?

DAVID – THE MADMAN

That day David fled from Saul and went to Achish king of Gath. But the servants

of Achish said to him, "Isn't this David, the king of the land? Isn't he the one they sing about in their dances?

"Saul has slain his thousands, and David his tens of thousands?"

David took these words to heart and was very much Afraid of Achish king of Gath.

1 Samuel 21:10-12

How is it that David could be Afraid of some king of Gath? Let's remember that we are talking about David, who as a young man was anointed by Samuel the prophet under the choosing and direction of GOD HIMSELF to be king of Israel. Let's take a short journey with David's life to help understand how this could happen and as we do, consider some of the steps or events in our own personal life that we can relate to through David.

When Samuel anointed David the SPIRIT of the LORD came upon David in power.

David, a shepherd boy was known as a brave man and a warrior.

David rescued his sheep from a lion and a bear and subsequently killed both.

David was called into King Saul's service because of his gifting in playing the harp.

David took on the uncircumcised Philistine Goliath, who had defied the armies of the living GOD, and killed him, then cut off Goliath's head with a sword.

David entered into a covenant relationship with King Saul's son Jonathan.

Whatever King Saul gave David to do he did it so successfully that David was given a high rank in the army.

The women danced and sang "Saul has slain his thousands, and David his tens of thousands" and all Judah and Israel loved David because he led them in their campaigns.

David married Saul's daughter Micah and continued to have more success in battles.

You talk about a man on the move that has it all going for him and David certainly has to fit that description. How is it then that David could go from his success story to eventually going into the enemy's camp and because he was Afraid of Achish King of Gath, he acted like a madman and pretended to be insane making marks on the doors of the gate and letting saliva run down his beard? It doesn't quite add up so let's continue to follow David's journey.

While David was having all his success and his fame continued to grow, King Saul became jealous of David to the point that Saul attempted to kill David and told his son Jonathan and all of Saul's attendants to kill David and David had to flee for his life. It is important to remember that when you are anointed by the LORD there will be others who may have envy or be jealous. In Mark's Gospel the LORD HIMSELF experienced this envy, even Pilate knew JESUS was handed over to him by the chief priests out of envy.

Let's now look at what David ultimately lost before he actually became the King of Israel and recognize what we, like Joseph, David and the others might lose before we walk in destiny and inheritance.

1. His covenant friendship with his dear friend Jonathan who lost his life in battle.
2. His mentor, the prophet Samuel.
3. His position and acclaim in the army.
4. His prestige among the people.
5. His marriage, as Saul gave his daughter to another man.
6. His friend Ahimelech, the priest who was killed along with 84 other priests.

It is easy to read about David's losses, but unless you have experienced these types of losses or personalize what effect it would have on you, it is just a story. It is important for us to know that there can be a call of GOD of destiny upon our life, and at some point in our journey everything will appear to go completely wrong. Nothing will make sense and we enter deep spiritual warfare where we begin to question and doubt. What happened to David can just as easily happen to us. There is a difference between fear and danger. David went into survivor mode and then entered the enemy (Achish, King of Gath) camp. We too can resort to our old survivor patterns and techniques and slide into the enemy camp. David knew he was where he did not belong, "was Afraid" and had to put on an Oscar Academy performance to escape by pretending to be insane. So often when we are ready to pack it in and call it quits it can also be that the timing for our breakthrough is just upon us.

David did escape to the cave of Adullam and let's remember David's story started as a shepherd boy BUT GOD had an anointing and calling upon him.

David, so popular and loved, now by himself in a cave. Can you imagine what is going through David's mind? Now we see GOD at work in chapter 22 of 1 Samuel. "When his brothers and his father's household heard about it, they went down to him there. All those who were in distress or in debt or discontented gathered around him, and he became their leader. About four hundred men were with him." What a crew GOD gave to David to begin his real leadership program. After David's darkest hour, the LORD begins the building process in David's life.

To move forward in David's life; shortly after David's escape Ahimelech's son Abiathar came to David as he was also running from Saul and what did David advise him? "Don't be Afraid."

As we read in Psalm 56 you will see in v3 "When I am Afraid, I will trust in YOU and in v4 and 10, 11, these words, 'In GOD I trust; I will not be Afraid. What can a mortal man do to me?"

May we be like David and "Don't be Afraid." May our fear turn to faith in GOD and HIS faithfulness.

ISAIAH - AHAZ

Say to him, 'Be careful, keep calm and Don't be Afraid. Do not lose heart because of these two smoldering stubs of firewood – because of the fierce anger of Rezin and Aram and of the son of Remaliah.
Isaiah 7:4

The LORD has instructed the prophet Isaiah to meet Ahaz the King of Judah because Ahaz and his people had heard a bad report about a plot against them and their hearts were shaken as trees of the forest are shaken by the wind. Any of us who have been in a forest during a time of a real wind storm can understand how their hearts must have been affected.

Ahaz came from the lineage of David and it is most interesting and strategic that later in this chapter, the LORD speaks directly to Ahaz to build up his faith and invites Ahaz to ask for a sign. Ahaz self-righteously states that he will not put the LORD to the test and the prophet Isaiah challenges him as a representative of the House of David that he not only is testing the patience of man but now also GOD. Isaiah continues on and speaks prophetically in v14. "Therefore, the LORD HIMSELF will give you a sign: The virgin will be with child and will give birth to a SON and will call him IMMANUEL." In the heart of the LORD, HE wanted to share the sign of IMMANUEL with Ahaz whose lineage was through the line of David, but Ahaz didn't want to "test the LORD." May we learn from this to walk in obedience and just how much HE wants to share HIS heart with us as well.

Isn't it amazing how much GOD wants to talk but we don't want to hear? Why do you think that is? HE knows our heart and that is the message you and I are giving HIM, as HE knows what is in our heart and not the verbal communication we like to give HIM that makes us feel good. Just before the LORD instructed Isaiah in our referenced scripture Chapter 7: 4 you will find Isaiah saying in:

Isaiah 6:8 Then I heard the voice of the LORD saying, "Whom shall I send?" And who will go for us?" And I said, "Here am I. Send me!" 'GOD is always looking, always searching for those who are willing to respond. Are you really willing to respond without the LORD first giving you all the details so you can prayerfully discern the proper response from your perspective? Unfortunately, GOD does not always work that way and as we see with Isaiah his response was unconditional and so should ours be.

In any case, one of Isaiah's assignments was to speak to King Ahaz of Judah. Clearly the LORD was going to deal with King Rezin of Aram (Syria) and Pekah, the son of Remaliah from Israel, the northern kingdom at the time and of course the LORD did deal with them. Maybe the LORD has an assignment for you to speak to someone, but HE is looking for your unconditional response first.

What we have here is an illustration of being "Afraid "and also the sensitivity of the LORD as these key principles are communicated.

1. Be careful.
2. Keep calm.
3. Don't be Afraid.
4. Do not lose heart.

When we are Afraid, it is fear that binds us in so many ways and one of those ways is we lose heart. We can see from scripture how the LORD keeps referring to our heart and when we lose heart we are on dangerous ground. When we face up to our fears in CHRIST, we find our freedom in CHRIST. So remember, "Do not be afraid."

ISAIAH - SALVATION

Strengthen the feeble hands, steady the knees that give way; say to those with Fearful hearts, "Be strong, Do not Fear; your GOD will come, HE will come with vengeance; with divine retribution HE will come to save you"

Then will the eyes of the blind be opened and the ears of the deaf unstopped.
Then will the lame leap like a deer and the mute tongue shout for joy.
Water will gush forth in the wilderness and streams in the desert.
Isaiah 35:3-6

Do you have a Fearful heart? Or better yet, do you know if you have a Fearful heart? GOD has given a solution with a promise.

Be strong.
Do not Fear.

The promise is the coming of the LORD not just referring to the first time or HIS return the second time which we all await but it is HIS coming moment by moment day by day.

HE will come to save us, and HE does which is HIS Ministry as the MESSIAH on earth. It is easy to say, "Be strong and do not Fear," but our GOD goes another step and HE gives us a promise of the Messiah and our redemption. Because HE has given HIS promise and we chose to believe, it builds us up so that in trusting in HIS promise we can "Be strong and not Fear." Belief in HIS promise is faith.

On a personal basis, I can so clearly remember the LORD calling me and wooing me into the arms of HIS love and into HIS kingdom. I was 33 years of age, had most of everything in life, had been able to experience so much in life and yet I was spiritually bankrupt. I had been presented with a salvation message and had no problem believing that JESUS CHRIST was the MESSIAH, YESHUA, and SAVIOR of the world. The issue that convicted me that I couldn't handle was that I was to make this historical SAVIOR, LORD of my life. Salvation – yes, LORDSHIP – there was no way!! As the HOLY SPIRIT continued to work deep in my life, the stumbling block was LORDSHIP. How do you, when you literally have almost everything you could ever dream of, turn it and your future decisions over to this historical SAVIOR? What happens if HE isn't really intimately involved in all of you, your daily decisions and your future? What happens if JESUS is only a historical JESUS and not a living intimate and real, personal LORD? I had searched for and experienced so much in my life and without consciously realizing it, if that truth of LORDSHIP was not real then there was no real truth. One day as I was walking on the beach, I kept trying to think of something I had not done or experienced and all of a sudden, this voice said: "John, stop running, I love you." I was totally freaked and tried to speed up my walk and again these words, "John, stop running. I love you." I of course, did not realize I was running from HIM, but HE knew my heart and spoke a promise and gift of love and LORDSHIP. Was it a lack of faith that I had or was it Fear that

HE really was not a living, intimate LORD that loved me so much that HE gave his life for me and my sins? Wherever you are, 'Don't be Afraid,' because HE is above everything totally real, trustworthy and loves you. HE loves to hear our heart saying to Him, "LORD JESUS, as my SAVIOR, please forgive me of my sins, I yield to you and your LORDSHIP. Come into my heart and life. I submit to you and please make me into what you desire. Teach me your ways and guide me into really knowing YOU and being able to honestly trust YOU. Amen."

If that is your prayer, then: Your blind eyes will be opened, and your deaf ears will be unstopped. You will jump like a deer for joy, your tongue will be loosened, so you will be able to praise HIS HOLY NAME and living water will gush through you. Shortly after giving my life to JESUS CHRIST I was going for a jog and for the first time I could hear the birds chirping like an orchestra and I started to weep realizing the beauty HE had created and how I had been so deaf to it. "Don't be Afraid". Just as I have shared my step of faith when HE came into my life, filled me with the precious HOLY SPIRIT and took a life full of the so called world's success but deep inside spiritually bankrupt and put HIS purpose inside me, HE will also do the same for you. Don't be Afraid. Just ask HIM.

ISAIAH – MY CHILDREN

"Do not be Afraid, for I am with you; I will bring your children from the east and gather you from the west I will say to the north, "Give them up!" and to the south, "Do not hold them back." Bring MY sons from afar and MY daughters from the ends of the earth – everyone who is called by MY NAME, whom I created for MY GLORY, whom I formed and made."

Isaiah 43:5-7

When GOD is about to do something significant, HE loves to prepare us and because it is significant, HE also let's us know there is no need: "To be Afraid". At times, it is to an individual person, a remnant, or in this particular case it was the nation of Israel. HE was using the prophet Isaiah to share the message.

As you examine this scripture, place a circle around every time you see the word 'I'. Then every time you see the word "MY', place a square around it.

Then every time you are instructed what you are to do, underline the specific instructions.

Note what HE is going to do.

I am with you

I will bring your children

and gather you

I will say to the north

and to the south

Bring MY sons

and MY daughters

I created

I formed

I made

Examine the relationships: MY sons, MY daughters, MY NAME, and MY GLORY. How can we not desire to bring glory to HIS name and to totally live for HIM unconditionally? Only GOD can do what HE states HE is going to do and right up front HE let's them know HE is with them, to give them comfort and assurance after HE has told them Not to be Afraid.

 What does HE tell us today? I will never leave you nor forsake you. I love it when HE owns what HE is going to do with us.   A few years after finally accepting and receiving the forgiveness and love of JESUS CHRIST, I had a most unique conversation with HIM that has served me as a key foundation in my spiritual journey with HIM.   I had a good understanding of the Christian ways or reaching the world and had come up with a couple of "new" ideas of how to reach the lost which was and is the cry of my heart.

One day in prayer, I was telling the LORD of my ideas and to my total surprise after sharing my first idea and asking HIM what HE thought, the sweet whisper of the LORD said "yes" and so I quickly added my second idea and again I heard that loving voice, "yes." You have to realize, as I did in hindsight, my ideas were not very good but when you have GOD'S attention, you go for it. I had what I thought were four good ideas but with HIS loving response after each idea, I quickly thought up three other ideas and HIS response was always the same. I couldn't come up with any other ideas so I asked "Well LORD, what do you think?" Because of each of HIS loving responses, I assumed I was on a roll and HE liked my ideas. HIS answer made me realize HE loved my heart for the lost but not necessarily my ideas as HE said "John, those are good, but watch what I am going to do." The simple truth is that HE has the plans and ideas which keep me in intimacy with HIM as I have desperately tried to be obedient to what HE wants done. What is most important for the Body of CHRIST is that we yield to HIM and let him be LORD not only of our lives, but our marriages, our relationships, the Churches, the Ministries, as HE has HIS plans and strategies to extend HIS Kingdom. What HE is doing is looking for those of us who will walk in obedience to what HE is instructing us to do. The one thing we are instructed to do: "Do not be Afraid" as it is all about HIM and HIS GLORY.

ISAIAH - HEARING

"Hear ME, you who know what is right, you people who have MY law in your hearts:

Do not Fear the reproach of men or be Terrified by their insults.

Isaiah 51:7

Isaiah whose name means "The LORD saves" is the son of Amoz and biblical scholars acknowledge Isaiah is the greatest of the writing prophets whose writing was during the expansion of the Assyrian empire and the decline of Israel.

In Isaiah 51:7, notice the LORD was crying "Hear ME" to those who knew what was right. Isn't it also true for followers of JESUS CHRIST today, that we need to hear HIM, in other words, at least be open to listen? For those of us who live in the western world who can freely and openly love the LORD, who are not really persecuted, would it be safe to say that if we really passionately and openly loved the LORD with all our hearts, souls and minds, that we might be considered odd, that we might receive insults, that it might cost us promotions, ridicule or more.   Look at Stephen. In fact, almost all the Apostles paid with their lives.   It cost our LORD everything and yet out of love for the whole world, including our own neighbours, HE gave HIS will and HIS life and maybe that is why HE also added that we are to love our neighbours as ourselves. HE lived and died what HE preached. HIS desire for all of our love has a cost attached to it.

Have you ever considered why we have not heard from the LORD? Have we earnestly sought HIM? Do we really believe that HE is intimately desirous of being totally involved in every detail of our life? Do we need to re-examine our relationship with HIM?

Are we open vessels for the LORD to speak to or do we need a burning bush or mule to talk to us to get our attention?   HE is not restricted by HIS communication methods so those who are good at the blame game can not blame HIM but have to look at ourselves.

When JESUS before HIS ascension met with HIS eleven disciples in Galilee, at the mountain where HE had told them to go, there were some of the disciples who doubted (isn't that comforting to those of us who are doubters), and gave HIS final instructions to both them and us in the Gospel of Matthew:

Then JESUS came to them and said" "All Authority in heaven and on earth has been given to ME. Therefore, go and make disciples of all nations, baptizing them in the name of the FATHER and of the SON and of the HOLY SPIRIT, and teaching them to obey everything I have commanded you. And surely, I am with you always, to the very end of the age" Matthew 28: 18-20

Those are pretty clear instructions but did HE really men "GO" and does that really apply to us in the 21st Century? "GO" is not just to the mission field because it is all around us but also includes going on our knees for the lost and winning the battle for them on our knees in prayer, or going to our neighbours, our employers, our fellow workers, our fellow students, our unsaved family members and yes we may be publicly insulted, embarrassed or threatened but HE did instruct us to "GO" with a promise which is simply, HE would always be with us

HIS instructions have an eternal perspective for those who know what is right and we can trust HIM when HE says, "Do not Fear."

JEREMIAH

But the LORD said to me, "Do not say, 'I am only a child.' You must go to everyone I send you to and say whatever I command you. Do not be Afraid of them, for I am with you and will rescue you," declares the LORD.

Then the LORD reached out HIS hand and touched my mouth and said to me, "Now I have put MY words in your mouth. See, today I appoint you over nations and kingdoms to uproot and tear down, to destroy and overthrow, to build and to plant."
Jeremiah 1:7-9

As we read this scripture, let your imagination place you in the place of Jeremiah the prophet and pretend you have just received this word from the LORD. How would you handle the instruction?

The good news is that our gracious LORD doesn't just throw a dart at our name but as we see, Jeremiah was set apart for GOD'S calling and purpose.

"Before I formed you in the womb I knew you, before you were born I set you apart; I appointed you as a prophet to the nations."
(Jeremiah 1:5)

We are all special to the LORD and have all been set apart for HIS purposes. I believe we have five challenges:

1. To seriously seek HIM for HIS calling and purpose for our lives.
2. To submit to HIM as the clay yields to the potter so we can be moulded and prepared for our destiny in HIM.
3. To be conformed in HIS image.
4. To Walk in obedience to HIM, and not our own understanding
5. To Trust HIM

In Jeremiah, who was called the 'weeping prophet' or the prophet of doom because of the nature of his message we have a special and unique man of GOD. How would you like to be known as a prophet of doom? On one hand we see the LORD referring to him as a fortified city and an iron pillar to stand against the whole land. On the other hand, in spite of the prophet's strong message against sin Jeremiah loved the people of Judah and prayed for them even though the LORD had advised him not to bother as HE would not listen.

What I love about Jeremiah's prayers is that he identified himself in the sin of repentance and may we also when we pray for our communities and nation.   Jeremiah went through a period of persecution and imprisonment and at one point the LORD instructed Jeremiah not to marry and have children as judgement was coming. We can see that when the LORD first instructed Jeremiah and told Jeremiah "Do not be Afraid of them," it was a good word for a necessary work that the LORD required from Jeremiah. How many of us have told the LORD that our lives are not our own and HE can do with us as HE wants and really meant it.? How many of us could handle the word of the LORD given to Jeremiah? Wouldn't it be great to be told that we are to go where HE sends us and say what we are told?   What a calling to be appointed over nations and kingdoms to uproot and tear down, to destroy and overthrow, to build and to plant. The reality is that for Jeremiah and for us, we have these words of comfort from the LORD, "Do not be Afraid of them, for I am with you and will rescue you."

The LORD is faithful and knows what we need when HE gives us instructions. Just remember, "Do not be Afraid."

EZEKIAL

The people to whom I am sending you are obstinate and stubborn. Say to them, "This is what the SOVEREIGN LORD says". And whether they listen or fail to listen – for they are a rebellious house- they will know that a prophet has been among them. And you, son of man, Do not be Afraid of them or their words. Do not be Afraid though briers and thorns are all around you and you live among scorpions. Do not be Afraid of what they say or terrified by them, though they are a rebellious house.
Ezekiel 2: 4-6

But I will make you as unyielding and hardened as they are. I will make your forehead like the hardest stone, harder than flint. Do not be Afraid of them or terrified by them, though they are a rebellious house."
Ezekiel 3: 8-9

Wow what a word from the LORD to Ezekiel, who was a member of the priesthood, who was among the Jews exiled to Babylon by Nebuchadnezzar and while there Ezekiel received his call to be a Prophet. Ezekiel means "GOD is strong" and some of the keys to the messages he gave to the fellow exiles were related to divine judgement, Jerusalem would fall, the LORD'S comfort for HIS people, revival, restoration and the glorious future as per the LORD'S promise for HIS people.

It was while Ezekiel was by the Kebar River that the heavens were opened, and he saw visions of GOD. For those of us who might be skeptical of these visions, I believe it is important to state what the word says in part regarding what was revealed to Ezekiel and his response as was noted above in the referenced scriptures in Ezekiel chapters 2 and 3.

In Ezekiel 1: 26-28 Above the expanse over their heads was what looked like a throne of sapphire, and high above on the throne was a figure like that of a MAN. I saw that from what appeared to be HIS waist up HE looked like glowing metal, as if full of fire, and that from there down HE looked like fire;

and brilliant light surrounded HIM. Like the appearance of a rainbow in the clouds on a rainy day, so was the radiance around HIM. This was the appearance of the likeness of the GLORY of the LORD. When I saw it, I fell facedown, and I heard the voice of ONE speaking.

I happen to love Ezekiel's posture when seeing the GLORY of the LORD and in todays time what is our posture when we see the GLORY of the LORD? If you have not seen the Glory of the Lord, what do you think your posture would be? Let me ask then if you have had an encounter with the HOLY SPIRIT what was your posture and or mindset? If you have not had an encounter with the HOLY SPIRIT do you desire one? If not, why not?

The LORD in HIS grace let's Ezekiel know that the people Ezekiel will be sharing GOD'S word with are a stubborn and obstinate people, but that Ezekiel is "Not to be Afraid" and that when they lash out verbally at Ezekiel, the LORD's instruction is "Do not be Afraid."

Is that just a word for the exiles or could it also be a word from the LORD to us that we also can be a stubborn and obstinate people? Remember that if the LORD is calling you to speak out HIS word "Do not be Afraid."

DANIEL

A hand touched me and set me trembling on my hands and knees. He said, "Daniel, you who are highly esteemed, consider carefully the words I am about to speak to you, and stand up, for I have now been sent to you." And when he said this to me, I stood up trembling.

Then he continued, "Do not be Afraid, Daniel. Since the first day that you set your mind to gain understanding and to humble yourself before your GOD, your words were heard, and I have come in response to them."

Daniel 10:10-12

Again, the one who looked like a man touched me and gave me strength. "Do not be Afraid, O man highly esteemed," he said, "Peace! Be strong now; be strong." When he spoke to me, I was strengthened and said, "Speak, my LORD, since you have given me strength."

Daniel 10: 18-19

The book of Daniel is such an incredible read as it pertains to Daniel along with three other Jewish young men taken to Babylon before the fall of Jerusalem. Daniel was a man who had a proven track record of walking with GOD without compromise in a nation that clearly did not follow the ways or teaching of GOD. When we think of the book of Daniel (named Belteshazzar) we naturally go to the three friends of Daniel (Shadrach, Meshach, Abednego) from Judah being sent into the fiery furnace and coming out totally unharmed, of Daniel being sent into the lion's den for the night and not having a wound on him because as the King Darius stated "your GOD sent HIS angel to shut the mouths of the lions," and of course the end time prophecy written by Daniel which even today is held as accurate and yet to come about.

Daniel chose to make tough decisions in serving the GOD of HEAVEN. Daniel knew his GOD in an intimate way, was bold in his faith and not only spoke the word of GOD but he also clearly ensured that those in authority knew that it was only the

GOD of HEAVEN who could reveal mysteries and give interpretation to dreams, that it was not him. What is often over looked with Daniel because of his clear non-compromising decision making and faith is his heart for people and not just his three friends from Judah. Have you ever wondered why the LORD would choose a young man like Daniel to accomplish so much for HIM? It becomes clear that out of Daniel's faithful intimacy with the LORD, the LORD gave revelation and interpretation of dreams. Who would not want that same honor and trust from the LORD today because as scripture a state HE is the same yesterday, today and forever? It is clear that Daniel by the grace of GOD could understand visions and dreams of all kinds and when the LORD gave the mystery of the dream and interpretation of King Nebuchadnezzar the first thing Daniel did was to praise the GOD of HEAVEN and should not a part of his worship also be a part of ours as well:

Let's look at Daniel 2:22-23 HE reveals deep and hidden things; HE knows what lies in darkness, and light dwells with HIM. I thank and praise you. O GOD of my fathers: YOU have made known to me what we asked of YOU, YOU have made known to us the dream of the king.

Daniel like Joseph was placed in a position of authority by the king but Daniel's initial request that was granted by the king was to have his three friends made administrators of the province. He did not forget his friends.

Daniel was given a unique end time vision and it is important that we understand Daniels condition at this time found in Daniel 8:15-17 While I, Daniel, was watching the vision and trying to understand it, there before me stood one who looked like a man. And I heard a man's voice from the Ulai calling: "Gabriel, tell this man the meaning of the vision." As he came near the place where I was standing, I was terrified and fell prostrate, "Son of man" he said to me, "understand that the vision concerns the time of the end."

Also:
Daniel 8: 26-27 "The vision of the evenings and mornings that has been given you is true, but seal

up the vision, for it concerns the distant future." I, Daniel, was exhausted and lay ill for several days. Then I got up and went about the king's business. I was appalled by the vision; it was beyond understanding.

Daniel was a man of the word and during the first year of king Darius reign Daniel understood the desolation of Jerusalem would last seventy years and similar to Nehemiah, Daniel pleaded in prayer and petition with fasting in sackcloth and ashes began to confess the sins and intercede for the Jewish people. Why Daniel? When have we had such a concern for the people of our communities and countries that we like Daniel will be so broken that we also will plead with the LORD in fasting and prayer? The LORD never asked Daniel to undertake the intercession, but HE knew Daniel's heart. What is in ours? We need to read the 9th Chapter of Daniel to fully understand the cry of Daniel's heart to the LORD. Daniel was a man who knew the LORD but knew he was just a servant of the LORD, confessed his own sin and the sin of the LORD'S people and knew true intercession. May we as HIS people use his intercession as a template.

Why then would Daniel, when touched by the man who is described in Daniel 10:5, 6 similarly described by the Apostle John, in Revelation 1:13-15 begin to tremble on his hands and knees and also stand up trembling? Note that Daniel bowed his face and was speechless until the one who looked like a man touched his lips and only then could Daniel address him as LORD. We also get a unique insight into the spiritual warfare where the prince of the Persian Kingdom resisted the "man" for 21 days until Michael the archangel helped him to be set free. We are also given a peek into the supernatural and the message to Daniel is personal and intimate.

Let's remember that this visitation was in response to Daniel:

1. Setting his mind to gain understanding.
2. Humbling himself before his LORD.
3. His prayers.
4. Being highly esteemed.
5. His care for his three friends

6. His intercession for a nation of people

I believe we see that when Daniel is having this incredible, beautiful encounter that has left him trembling and speechless, the words "Don't be Afraid' were spoken to help him receive the messenger and the message.   This was further confirmed in Daniel 10:18, 19; Again the one who looked like a man touched me and gave me strength. "Do not be Afraid, O man highly esteemed," he said. "Peace! Be strong now; be strong." When he spoke to me, I was strengthened and said, "Speak, my LORD, since YOU have given me strength."

What an honor to be referred to as "O man highly esteemed." Our GOD is so faithful that when HE has something unique for us to do, or when HE has something HE wants to share with us or reveal to us, HE helps us to receive it by "Do not be Afraid."

ZECHARIAH

"As you have been an object of cursing among the nations, O Judah and Israel, so will I save you, and you will be a blessing. Do not be Afraid, but let your hands be strong."

This is what the LORD ALMIGHTY says: "Just as I had determined to bring disaster upon you and showed no pity when your fathers angered me," says the LORD ALMIGHTY, "so now I have determined to do good again to Jerusalem and Judah. Do not be Afraid."

Zechariah 8:13-15

Zechariah is not only a prophet but also a priest whose name means "The LORD (YAHWEH) Remembers". It is written during the time of the Jewish restoration from Babylon captivity and he was among those who returned to Judah. Zechariah is one of the twelve "Minor Prophets" and we need to remember that the messages of the Minor Prophets are noted more for the length than their importance. In fact, the book of Zechariah has so much "meat" in it that you need to consider it as a must read. I will highlight a couple special scriptures that have spoken to me such as: 1. Israel being the apple of HIS eye, 2. the LORD is jealous for Jerusalem and Zion, 3. "Not by might nor by power but by my SPIRIT", 4. "who despises the day of small things", 5. "Administer true justice; 6. show mercy and compassion to one another" , 7. "Do not oppress the widow or the fatherless, the alien or the poor, 8. in your hearts do not think evil of each other". In particular Chapter 14 which proclaims the MESSIAH'S coming and HIS kingdom when HE will stand on the Mount of Olives, (you need to go there) east of Jerusalem, when the LORD will be King over the whole earth. On that day there will be one LORD and HIS NAME the ONLY NAME, and the yearly worship and celebration on the Feast of Tabernacles.

Clearly one of Zechariah's messages is to motivate the people of Judah to complete the rebuilding of the temple. The LORD through Zechariah in Chapter 8 is obviously speaking to Judah and Israel, not directly to a person but there are some key principles that are relevant to us as well. We read the heart and love of the LORD for Jerusalem and HIS blessings upon Jerusalem which will be called the City of Truth, and the Holy Mountain. As the nations violated the things of GOD, they came under cursing of the nations. As individuals, when we embrace sin and do not deal with it by turning to the LORD in true repentance, we become exposed to the enemy. Our lives become one of deceit and shame and a pattern develops. As the LORD saved Judah and Israel, they in turn would be a blessing. It is no different for us. When we turn back to the LORD in humility and brokenness, we too become a blessing. Why then would the LORD state, "Do not be Afraid"? When transformation takes place, nations need to be delivered from the bondage of being cursed and we need to be set free (inner healing) from deceit and shame. Being set free is a major adjustment and thus the reality "Do not be Afraid" to assist and encourage us in our transformation transitioning.

Many Christians wonder what inner healing refers to and I trust some of these subjects will assist:

Wounds from the past

Shame

Demonic oppression

Survival patterns

Sins of others and subsequent crisis

Ungodly beliefs

Unforgiveness

Self Image.

The LORD shares HIS heart and HIS ways by letting them also know how HE was grieved by their fathers but as this scripture states, GOD determines to do good, and we must learn "Don't be Afraid." HE can truly be trusted in every way.

MARY & JOSEPH

The angel went to her and said, "Greetings, you are who are highly favored! The LORD is with you."

Mary was greatly troubled at his words and wondered what kind of greeting this might be. But the angel said to her, "Do not be Afraid, Mary, you have found favour with GOD. You will be with child and give birth to a SON, and you are to give him the name JESUS."

Luke 1:28-31

When GOD decides to do something significant through us, our lives will never be the same and although the illustration of the encounter between Mary and the angel Gabriel was an extreme, our lives can change that quickly.

Mary, who was in Nazareth looking forward to her marriage to Joseph, is confronted by the angel and his words, and as we read, she was troubled by his words and wondered what kind of greeting this might be. Mary clearly had a balance between where we see she didn't just freely embrace what had taken place, but she didn't run from it either. The angel was sent to her to give her this incredible message that she was to become the Mother of the CHRIST child but before the angel could give her all the details these key words were spoken to her "Don't be Afraid, Mary." The angel did not give her the process, the favour of GOD, the encouragement of her relative Elizabeth being pregnant with child and the statement that is as real today as then that nothing is impossible with GOD, the angel needed to help her receive all of this with these key words, "Do not be Afraid, Mary".

At certain times if we have fear, we are unable to receive let alone process and reason what the message is about. In this particular case the words "Do not be Afraid Mary" probably had a dual purpose.

1. Allowing Mary to hear and begin to understand the message.
2. Preparing her in some manner for the days that were ahead for her.

Let's be real and agree that a young teenage girl engaged to be married living at that time in Nazareth, a town in Galilee, with her family and neighbours with no sexual contact with her fiancé tells her family, friends and even her fiancé that she is pregnant through the power of the HOLY SPIRIT probably needed the words "Do not be Afraid, Mary."

As we know Mary visited her relative Elizabeth who was also pregnant and by the grace and faithfulness of our LORD, Mary had to be encouraged when Elizabeth's child (John the Baptist) still in her womb leaped when he heard Mary's greeting. Elizabeth was filled with the HOLY SPIRIT and spoke these prophetic words under the unction of the HOLY SPIRIT: Luke 1: 42- 45 In a loud voice she exclaimed: "Blessed are you among women, and blessed is the CHILD you will bear! But why am I so favored, that the mother of my LORD should come to me? As soon as the sound of your greeting reached my ears, the baby in my womb leaped for joy. Blessed is she who has believed that what the LORD has said to her will be accomplished!" What a confirmation to Mary that what was said to her by the angel was in fact going to be a reality and what an encouragement from the LORD that she was blessed because she believed. Little did Mary realize that some 700 years before this encounter Isaiah spoke these prophetic words to the House of David who were looking for a sign. Isaiah 7: 14 "Therefore the LORD HIMSELF will give you a sign: The virgin will be with child and will give birth to a SON, and will call HIM IMMANUEL." Let's remember that true prophecy must be confirmed in the word just as Isaiah's prophecy. We can see the abuse of "self" prophecy today but let's honor the correct prophecy.

Let us take a look at how the LORD prepared Joseph, who was to be the human father for the raising of the CHRIST child. To keep it in perspective, both Mary and Joseph were receiving a message from far different worldly perspectives. Mary, a virgin, was told that the child was conceived from the HOLY SPIRIT and Joseph who had no intimate relationship with Mary being told she was with child through the HOLY SPIRIT.

In the Gospel of Matthew, we read 'Because Joseph her husband was a righteous man and did not want to expose her to public disgrace, he had in mind to divorce her quietly. But after he had considered this, an angel of the LORD appeared to him in a dream and said, "Joseph son of David, Do not be Afraid to take Mary home as your wife, because what is conceived in her is from the HOLY SPIRIT. She will give birth to a son, and you are to give him the name JESUS, because HE will save HIS people from their sins."' *(Matthew 1:19, 20)* This scripture tells us something of the quiet character of Joseph that before the angel spoke to Joseph in a dream, he was trying not to expose Mary to public disgrace, and he figured that a quiet divorce would within reason protect her. We must understand the culture of the times, but let's be honest men that the normal pattern for men today would be to cut and run? Joseph was trying to be sensitive and protective when many would perceive that he did not need to be. Now we see the intervention of the LORD by an angel of the LORD who appears to Joseph in a dream and reveals to Joseph the full picture about Mary, to take Mary as his wife, her pregnancy, the birth of the son to be named JESUS and JESUS's destiny for those who will become HIS people. Again, we see the angel of the LORD sharing these key words to Joseph, "Do not be Afraid." The action of Joseph speaks so much to his faith, character, integrity and obedience to the LORD.

As with everything, when the LORD gives us something, there are two parts:
1. His message.
2. Our response.

Before we look at Mary and Joseph's response, what would our response be if we were them and more to the point, what was our response to the last thing the HOLY SPIRIT told us to do?

In Joseph's case, when he woke up, he did what the angel of the LORD had commanded him and took Mary as his wife (*Matthew 1:24*). Mary's response in Luke 1:38: "I am the LORD'S servant," Mary answered. "May it be to me as you have said." Then the angel left her.

The words spoken to both Mary and Joseph probably carried them on their journey from Nazareth to Bethlehem because it is not a short walk but in fact a real tough journey. Interestingly Bethlehem means "House of Bread" and HE who was born in Bethlehem is the "Bread of Life." After such a trying journey while there might be differences of exactly where JESUS was born we can all correctly agree that the birth of JESUS was a unexpected challenge for Mary and Joseph and shortly thereafter an angel of the LORD appears to Joseph telling him to take Mary and JESUS to Egypt as Herod is looking to kill JESUS. What a journey of faith and obedience Mary and Joseph teach us.

Both Mary and Joseph challenge us with their unconditional faith and obedience. Why Mary and Joseph? Faith is to trust in HIM and HIS word with obedience. We also have a great illustration of our LORD'S faithfulness to communicate the key words of trust and encouragement so we can receive and obey, "Do not be Afraid."

THE GHOST

During the fourth watch of the night JESUS went out to them, walking on the lake. When the disciples saw HIM walking on the lake, they were terrified. "It's a ghost," they said, and cried out in Fear.

But JESUS immediately said to them: "Take courage! It is I. Don't be Afraid."

Matthew 14:25-27

Twelve macho men hand picked by the LORD, of which several were fishermen sitting in a boat watching JESUS CHRIST walking on the lake and being terrified believing JESUS to be a ghost. As we read, they were so terrified, they cried out in Fear. As we know before the event, JESUS made the disciples get into the boat and go ahead of him to the other side while he dismissed the crowd that HE had been teaching. As we examine the scriptures where the LORD or HIS Angels are telling bible characters to "Don't be Afraid", it is before HE gives them instructions or tasks they are about to experience but in this case HE does the supernatural and we see their expression of Fear.

It is important to remember that JESUS had just fed the 5,000 from 5 loaves of bread and two fish and after everyone had eaten to the point they were satisfied, the disciples picked up 12 basketfuls of broken pieces that were left over. The disciples had just seen the supernatural at work and yet here they are, on the boat crying out in fear. It is hard to imagine what was actually going on with them that they would be so terrified. If we follow JESUS' steps, we realize after HE had instructed the disciples to get into the boat and go to the other side, HE dismissed the crowd and HE went up the mountainside by HIMSELF to pray. We also know that JESUS never did anything but what the FATHER had showed HIM, so it makes sense that JESUS was trying to teach the disciples about the supernatural and it was beyond their level of faith, belief or understanding. HE also tried to teach them about HIS death and subsequent resurrection, and they had problems with that, so like us, they were in a learning mode. JESUS identifies HIMSELF to HIS disciples and tells them to take courage and "Don't be Afraid."

Our dear brother Peter of course getting an assurance from JESUS that it is in fact HIM takes JESUS at HIS word, gets out of the boat and starts walking on the lake until he saw the wind and was " Afraid " and begins to sink and cries out to the LORD. JESUS, of course, reached out HIS hand and caught him and makes this amazing statement: "You of little faith," HE said, "Why did you doubt?"

This exercise is a teaching on faith in JESUS CHRIST and only HIM. We can't walk in faith "being Afraid". While we focus on Peter and what happened to him it is important for us to also focus on the disciples who did not even get out of the boat. Who do you identify with? Are you a Peter? Or are you still in the boat?

We cannot put our LORD in our little spiritual box of understanding when HE is trying to enlarge our faith. Let's remember that HE has supernaturally fed the 5,000 and we see HIM now walking on water. We can love those stories because we were not there and did not experience the supernatural at work, so we are safe in reading the stories. What happens to our theology when the HOLY SPIRIT tries to get our attention and we wrongly harden our heart, mind and theology and discreetly back off HIS PRESENCE? It is sad to hear believers state "it has to be in the word" or it is not from the LORD. We have just highlighted scriptures of the feeding of the 5,000 and JESUS walking on water so let's agree the LORD is breaking down the theology of HIS disciples and hopefully ours as HE does the supernatural and places it in HIS word for us. Whatever HE speaks to us HE confirms it in HIS word so it will line up with scripture, but it is not our place to tell the LORD the "only way" we will accept something from HIM is when we read it in the word. Who is LORD and who wants to be in control? Shame! When we next encounter HOLY SPIRIT in a supernatural way, just remember to be open to HIM and "Do not be Afraid."

MARYS

The angel said to the women, "Do not be Afraid, for I know that you are looking for JESUS, who was crucified. HE is not here; HE has risen, just as HE said. Come and see the place where HE lay."

Matthew 28:5, 6

Mary Magdalene and the other Mary went to the tomb and encountered an angel from the LORD who is described as having an appearance like lightning and HIS clothes were white as snow. The first part of the statement the angel made to the Marys was: "Do not be Afraid"

We see that when the angel had appeared to the guards at the tomb. They were so Afraid of him they shook and became like dead men. Our first inclination might be that the two Marys would be Afraid of him as well, however, it becomes clear that the angel was preparing them for the truth; that the tomb was indeed empty, as JESUS had risen from the dead and they were to tell the disciples and then go to Galilee. This encounter the Marys had with the Angel was indeed significant to them, the disciples, and subsequently, you and me. Do you ever wonder why the two Marys were the first people to have received the truth of our risen SAVIOR? There are no coincidences with GOD and the two Marys having received this truth is not a coincidence.

As the Marys were going to tell the disciples the scripture states they were "Afraid yet filled with joy" (*Matthew 28:8*). As they carried on their way, they then met JESUS, clasped HIS feet and worshipped HIM. 'Then JESUS said to them, "Do not be Afraid. Go and tell MY brothers to go to Galilee; there they will see ME."' (*Matthew 28:10*). I love their response of love and emotion expressed to our precious SAVIOR and can't you imagine the pleasure our SAVIOR received from them? What would our response be if we were one of the Marys?

You would wonder why JESUS would tell the Marys "Do not be Afraid" but these two ladies are so emotionally filled with joy and also trying to work through the key to Christianity, which is the death and resurrection of our precious SAVIOR, JESUS CHRIST. Isn't it interesting that JESUS CHRIST instructs these two ladies to go to the disciples and inform them that they are to go to Galilee, and it is in Galilee where they will see HIM? These mighty disciples, except the Apostle John, had scattered when JESUS was arrested, beaten and crucified and now they had to take this long trek from Jerusalem to Galilee. Can you imagine the theological discussions they had on this long walk even though JESUS had taught them of HIS death and resurrection? What has JESUS tried to teach you and me that we have still not understood and as a result it distorts our truth in HIS teachings?

By the way, if you have never been to Israel, I can not encourage you enough to go if at all possible, as it will have a major significance in your walk with GOD and understanding of scripture. Trust me; the walk from Jerusalem to Galilee is not a fifteen minute walk. There are times in our lives when we can be overwhelmed by a move of our LORD but one of the keys to help us work through the issues is "Do not be Afraid." The key according to the angel for the Marys and the key for us as well is they were looking for JESUS and we need to always be looking for HIM as well. When HE appears to us out of our traditional, safe comfort zone let us remember "Do not be Afraid."

JESUS IN THE BOAT

JESUS was in the stern, sleeping on a cushion. The disciples woke HIM and said to HIM, "TEACHER, don't YOU care if we drown?"

HE got up, rebuked the wind and said to the waves, "Quiet, be still!" Then the wind died down and it was completely calm.

HE said to HIS disciples, "Why are you so Afraid? Do you still have no faith?"

They were terrified and asked each other, "Who is this? Even the wind and the waves obey HIM!"

Mark 4:38-41

What a contrast JESUS gives to HIS disciples between faith and fear. The disciples did not have the big picture of the big GOD we love, serve and know. It is one thing to be with JESUS when HE healed people, when HE drove out evil spirits and when HE taught but it is another matter to see HIM rebuke the wind and speak to the waves and have them obey Him.

The disciples' theology got thrown out the window to the point their question was "Who is this?" A question for us – what is our perspective or understanding of our LORD? Many of us in trying to satisfy our intellectual understanding of our LORD actually, in most cases innocently bring HIM down to our mind set, which gives us comfort and over a period of time prevents us from total surrender to really know HIM. It actually minimizes our faith and trust in HIM. For those who can not surrender and truly trust the LORD, the issues of control and manipulation become distorted and reversed. The disciples at this point did not have the revelation of "the word became flesh", the full understanding of the Trinity, the death and resurrection, nor had they yet experienced Pentecost, so their body of knowledge of the omnipresent, omnipotent, indescribable GOD was limited. Again, the question for us is: what is our perspective of the LORD? Do we really believe in HIS omnipresence, or HIS omnipotence? The question is; have we experienced this indescribable LORD and then the remaining question is do we really desire the fullness of this indescribable LORD?

On a personal basis, I had a unique experience within a month of my salvation that has helped me in understanding our limitations in knowing HIM. As a businessman (before the word marketplace became the 'catch all phrase'), I was attempting to have the LORD confirm HIS calling and purpose for my life. I was under a lot of pressure from well meaning friends to go to Bible school and become a Pastor or go to Missions but in my limited relationship with the LORD I did not have peace and in fact felt the LORD wanted me to stay in the business world. "By coincidence" I was going for lunch with a new client I had never met and for some reason sensed that this lunch was a confirmation of GOD'S leading for me. I also felt that I was to share my spiritual conversion and rebirth with this man. I was pretty excited until we sat down and the man in introducing his background explained that years before he had been a Minister. As I listened to him, I could tell he was a troubled, angry person but I also clearly heard he had gone to Bible school and had been an ordained Minister. It knocked the wind out of me, and I quickly prayed, "LORD forgive me, but I must have made a mistake. I thought I was to share my conversion, but this guy was a Minister and if I start talking, I am going to embarrass both YOU and myself. He obviously knows the Bible and I am still trying to figure out the books of the Old and New Testament. If he asks me any biblical questions, I am in trouble. Forgive me for my mistake." I thought I was off the hook until the LORD said to me, "John, you experienced MY forgiveness and love did you not?" and of course I quietly told the LORD "Absolutely" and then the LORD said "John, this man has an intellectual understanding of the Bible but has not experienced my forgiveness and love and I want you to share your personal experience as he needs to hear it." The next thing I know, I am sharing with this man my personal story and I see tears coming down his cheeks. He obviously had never experienced a heart transformation of falling in love with JESUS CHRIST, but in fact did a couple of months later. I quickly discovered the difference between knowing about and knowing HIM.

The disciples in that boat were being introduced to a new dimension of JESUS CHRIST that overwhelmed them and as we grow in HIM, we are supposedly being continually changed but so also so is our understanding of HIM as we get to know HIM better. Just take a moment and look back a year ago and tell the HOLY SPIRIT of the changes that have been made in your life – both the good and bad. Then let the HOLY SPIRIT know of the changes you would like to see HIM make in your life. GOD will do what we consider foolish acts to test us and stretch us and our faith such as speaking to the wind. HE is always, if we allow HIM desperately trying to expand our faith and trust in HIM even if it does not make sense to us. We must always remember HE will share HIS glory with no one. In our journey with the LORD, if we allow HIM, HE will put us into the boat and our faith will be challenged but let's remember fear can bind us so "Do not be Afraid."

ZECHARIAH

Then an angel of the LORD appeared to him, standing at the right side of the altar of incense. When Zechariah saw HIM, he was startled and was gripped with fear. But the angel said to him: "Do not be Afraid, Zechariah; your prayer has been heard. Your wife Elizabeth will bear you a son, and you are to give him the name John."

Luke 1:11-13

Zechariah was serving as a priest and as was the custom he was to go into the Temple of the LORD and burn incense while all the others were outside the Temple worshipping. The angel of the LORD continues sharing with Zechariah the calling and purpose of John but Zechariah was stuck at reasoning and could not move forward. It had been 400 years since Malachi had foretold of the person of John and Zechariah could not begin to receive and thus believe. It is covered in Luke 1: 17 And he will go on before the LORD, in the spirit and power of Elijah, to turn the hearts of the fathers to their children and the disobedient to the wisdom of the righteous - to make ready a people prepared for the LORD.

Zechariah could not believe in his own ability and thus was unable to have the faith to believe what GOD could do in spite of Zechariah and his wife Elizabeth's barren condition. Seems like a familiar story of doubt similar to Abraham and Sarah's. While Zechariah was visited by the angel of the LORD he was given words of comfort, "Do not be Afraid."

As a result of not believing the words of the Angel from the LORD, Zechariah was unable to speak until the birth of John. Interesting that while Elizabeth was pregnant with John she received a visit from Mary who was pregnant with our LORD, JESUS CHRIST and as noted in Luke1: 41 When Elizabeth heard Mary's greeting, the baby leaped in her womb, and Elizabeth was filled with the HOLY SPIRIT. As followers of JESUS CHRIST, there are times when the HOLY SPIRIT speaks something to us that reasoning cannot begin to fathom what is being said, but the presence of the HOLY SPIRIT and our spirit resonate, and it bypasses our reasoning.

 Unfortunately, many believers of JESUS CHRIST are bound by fear of the HOLY SPIRIT and thus cannot enter into full destiny and purpose. While angels are still a part of the spiritual dynamics today as they were in the Old Testament, the role of the HOLY SPIRIT, the third person of the Trinity confirmed with the word are our normal means of communication today.

The enemy has deceived many in the body of CHRIST about the HOLY SPIRIT who in scripture is described as our comforter, counselor, spirit of truth, teacher, intercessor, life-giver, revealer, etc, so of course there is spiritual war against the HOLY SPIRIT. It is clear that fear is a major weapon against believers and followers of our LORD of getting too close or intimate with the HOLY SPIRIT. Conversely, there can also be an abuse of the HOLY SPIRIT which causes confusion in the Body of CHRIST.

The FATHER and the SON in heaven and many of us look forward to the return of the SON to earth but in the wisdom of the GODHEAD, they have left the third person of the Trinity, which is the HOLY SPIRIT, here with us. We "Do not need to be Afraid" as HE is part of the Trinity and can be totally trusted. The fullness of the HOLY SPIRIT gives us power to be used of HIM. The fruit of the SPIRIT reflects the passion of JESUS CHRIST. The gifts of the HOLY SPIRIT are "gifts". Scripture states that we are to desire spiritual gifts. I don't know too many children that don't want 'gifts' from their parents. Scripture also states we are to have faith like children and come to the LORD as children. Why would we not want HIS gifts? Very early in my Christian walk, I was very desirous of the gifts of the SPIRIT, desiring them to be very much a part of my walk with HIM. While in earnest prayer, the most unique revelation came to me that I trust may help some readers. Out of nowhere I stated "LORD help me as I believe YOU are releasing YOUR gifts, but I am having problems unwrapping the gift package. As a result, I am not receiving the gifts YOU have for me. Please help me to unwrap the gifts, which HE did." May I encourage you to also desire and receive all HE has for you. You can trust HIM but remember, "Don't be Afraid."

SHEPHERDS

And there were shepherds living out in the fields nearby, keeping watch over their flocks at night. An angel of the LORD appeared to them, and the GLORY of the LORD shone around them, and they were terrified. But the angel said to them, "Do not be Afraid. I bring you good news of great joy that will be for all the people. Today in the town of David a SAVIOR has been born to you; HE is CHRIST the LORD."
Luke 2:8-11

So many of us can go through our journey of faith feeling that we have not made much of a difference and from time to time wonder how others seem to be set aside for unique spiritual purposes by the LORD while we carry on. Something like the shepherds in the field taking care of the sheep. Who would see them, who would recognize them for what they faithfully did day after day / night after night. Then all of a sudden their world totally changes and they have this incredible encounter with an angel of the LORD and the GLORY of the LORD shines around them.

We must recognize that these shepherds are not a bunch of wimps but real men who have been raised to protect the herd from all sorts of attacks which means they are prepared to fight for and defend the safety of these sheep, as it is a calling, a way of providing for not only them but their families and others.

Have you ever asked yourself why the LORD would choose these shepherds to share the Good News for all people that a SAVIOR has been born and HE is the CHRIST, the YESHUA, the MESSIAH, the LORD, the answer for the sins of the world, the bridge from man to the FATHER, the answer to all our questions. These uneducated men, smelling of sheep, not even having attended bible school are picked by the LORD to reveal this foretold miracle of HIS coming (first time) in the flesh. We can understand the heart of the LORD in HIS choosing as HE is our shepherd, has the heart of a shepherd and can relate to these shepherds. All of us who think we are overlooked from time to time can be encouraged that HE never overlooks our calling and purpose.

This encounter with the shepherds is not some ho hum event - it is orchestrated by the LORD HIMSELF in HIS Heavenly GLORY and these shepherds needed to hear these words "Don't be Afraid" because this was such a supernatural event that there was no way these shepherds were trained or prepared to handle such an event and such Good News. The angel confirms to them that they will find a baby wrapped in cloths and lying in a manger. There is an action item coming up and normally when the HOLY SPIRIT whispers something to us there is an action item about to happen if we are not frozen in disbelief or fear. In this case let's look at their initial response. Luke 2:15 When the angels had left them and gone into heaven, the shepherds said to one another, "Let's go to Bethlehem and see this thing that has happened, which the LORD has told us about." Take note of their confidence that this supernatural event in the fields was of the LORD and see both their confidence and steps of faith in actually going to see for themselves. They could have just as easily said to themselves "wow that was interesting but let's play this safe and stay here with the sheep."

They have now entered into their second action item in Luke 2: 16-17 So they hurried off and found Mary and Joseph, and the BABY, who was lying in the manger. When they had seen HIM, they spread the word concerning what had been told about this CHILD. In doing so they became the first evangelists in sharing the Good News and the question we have to ask ourselves is "do we really share the Good News" like the shepherds. They spread the word which was an action item for them and how can it not be an action item for us as well. If we really believe there is a heaven and hell, believing we have the Good News of the keys to eternal life, how can we not share? If we are really in love with JESUS CHRIST, how could we not share that love?

Not a bad night's work for some shepherds taking care of their sheep. No wonder they needed to hear, "Do not be afraid." I think what I love so much about this story is why the LORD would choose these shepherds to accomplish so much in such a short period of time. We know the LORD is our Shepherd. There is a protective, caring, serving attitude and personal make up that distinguishes a shepherd. No wonder these shepherds were chosen by the LORD to be the first to share the Good News.

What would our response have been if we had been a shepherd that night and told by an angel of the LORD that GOD had come to earth as a BABE born in a manger? Let's remember that JESUS CHRIST is coming back to earth (2ND TIME) and between now and then we should expect the unexpected.

If CHRIST is real in your life, how can you not share that reality? When CHRIST said in the great commission, "go", did HE really mean it? Are we that indifferent and uncaring? May the HOLY

SPIRIT set us free, so we do share the truth and that HIS life and death is not in vain for others. Remember,"Do not be Afraid."

JAIRUS

While JESUS was still speaking, someone came from the house of Jairus, the synagogue ruler. "Your daughter is dead," he said. "Don't bother the TEACHER anymore."

Hearing this, JESUS said to Jairus, "Don't be Afraid; just believe, and she will be healed."

Luke 8:49,50

We know very little about Jairus and what his belief truly was in JESUS except that he had a father's love for his daughter and had made a decision that her only hope of surviving was found in the person of JESUS CHRIST. Jairus, a ruler of the synagogue had come to JESUS and fell at JESUS' feet pleading that JESUS would come to his home because his twelve year old daughter was dying.

The authority, teaching, healing, deliverance and love of JESUS CHRIST had spread throughout Israel and people were being challenged in determining whether JESUS was the SON of GOD, the SAVIOR of the world, a prophet, a cult leader or any other spiritual target that was on their list. JESUS agreed to Jairus request and on his way to Jairus' home HE was intercepted on separate occasions. The first was an unnamed woman who had been subject to bleeding for twelve years, who came up behind JESUS when HE was walking and touched the edge of HIS cloak and she was immediately healed. JESUS response is found in Luke 8: 46 But JESUS said, "Someone touched ME; I know that power has gone from ME." Can we fully understand how in tune JESUS was with the healing anointing that HE carried that just by someone touching the edge of HIS cloak HE knew the power had left HIM? By JESUS stopping and addressing the matter the woman came forward falling at HIS feet explaining why she touched HIM and that she was immediately healed. That is a testimony! Can you imagine how the faith grew for those in the crowd when this miracle took place? The second interruption was from someone at Jairus home with the news that Jairus' daughter was dead. If you and I were Jairus, it would be a very normal reaction and emotion to feel grief, sadness, depression, sorrow and anger. JESUS doesn't address any of Jairus's grief feelings, but HE says to Jairus, "Don't be Afraid, just believe and she will be healed." In other words, JESUS was telling Jairus Not to be Afraid to prepare Jairus not to go into disbelief, shock or grief but to have faith in HIM because of what HE was about to do in spite of the report.

Dear reader, that is a powerful truth of the working, ways and truth of how HE is at work, so please "Don't be Afraid' to believe in HIM. It is consistent with scripture and was one of the keys from GOD for writing this book as the HOLY SPIRIT is trying to prepare us for what HE is about to do. In this particular case, JESUS is imparting faith in HIS resurrection power just as HE had imparted faith by healing the woman who touched the edge of HIS cloak. We need to be encouraged and let our faith blossom in HIM. When they arrive at Jairus' home, JESUS was very selective of who could come into Jairus's home besides the mother and father by inviting Peter, John and James. Let's note that JESUS kept all other unbelief out of Jairus house as the crowd were wailing and mourning and even after JEUS told them to stop, they laughed at HIM. We see at key supernatural times, JESUS reduces HIS mentoring and teaching to John, James and Peter instead of the twelve disciples as HE did at the Mount of Transfiguration and let's note those three became the Fathers of the early church.

JESUS resurrects Jairus' daughter and HE tells Jairus and his wife who were astonished not to tell anyone what had happened. JESUS knew that the people would have problems accepting HIS resurrection power of raising Jairus daughter from the dead and HE was very aware of the timing of HIS events. One of the keys for Jairus as well as for us is "believe". What is it in your life that JESUS wants you to believe for?

As JESUS spoke to Jairus, HE will also in the last days, speak to you and I as HE prepares us in advance of what HE is about to do, but let us remember "Don't be Afraid."

THE CROWD

"I tell you, MY friends, Do not be Afraid of those who kill the body and after that can do no more."
Luke 12:4

Indeed, the very hairs of your head are all numbered. Don't be Afraid; you are worth more than many sparrows.
Luke 12:7

Then JESUS said to HIS disciples: "Therefore I tell you, do not worry about your life, what you will eat; or about your body, what you will wear."
Luke 12:22

"Do not be Afraid, little flock, for your FATHER has been pleased to give you the kingdom."
Luke 12:32

The setting is JESUS teaching to a crowd of many thousands (that was before mega churches were mega churches) but first speaks to HIS disciples and as always, you need to read all of scripture in its proper context. However, when you read about one-half of a Chapter and see a consistent theme, "Do not be Afraid"; we need to push for understanding with "eyes to see" and "ears to hear". It is important for us to really understand the spiritual warfare we are a part of. As HIS children, it is very clear that the enemy does everything he can to divide and conquer, to distort the truth and have us question our LORD'S credibility, reliability, trustworthiness, HIS love and faithfulness. If someone gets in our face and challenges our faith, I trust we will stand strong, however in the subtle deceptive ways of the enemy, he does everything to ensure we have questions or doubts or hesitation in our LORD and who HE really is. HE tries to have us question the character of GOD.

The enemy does not waste time worrying about those of us who do not really have an intimate, personal relationship of love and trust in our LORD. What JESUS is teaching the disciples and us, is the real character of our GOD and introduces us to the Kingdom of GOD. HE helped the disciples and us to realize how precious we are and clearly is trying to encourage us to build up our own faith in HIM and HIS faithfulness. What JESUS teaches in clear repetitiveness is "Don't be Afraid' and "Do not Worry" because JESUS knows that until those issues are dealt with, there can be no real faith and trust in HIM. When fear and worry bind us there will be no real growth, which means destiny, inheritance, purpose and calling in HIM are not fulfilled. To be in denial that fear is not an issue appears to be contrary to scripture. GOD who created us is constantly saying in scripture, "Do not be Afraid." Our journey of faith should be a maturing, growing process of intimacy with GOD.

If you had to describe GOD to someone today and then a year from now describe GOD to the same person, I trust you would have a greater depth of knowing GOD than you did a year previous and be able to share the changes that HE has made in your life. This would include how you have fallen more in love with HIM, the details of how HE has worked in your life, how HE has given greater revelation to you of HIS word, how HE has opened doors for you to share of HIS love to the unsaved and how you have heard HIS still quiet voice.

I was travelling by plane on a short flight and have found that it is a place where HE places unsaved people next to me. In this case the passenger beside me was an unsaved lady with a Doctorate in Education and initially was very stand offish but eventually the conversation started and then turned spiritual. We initially were talking about her husband who was a well known figure and one that I had not met but knew that he was searching spiritually. As we talked, I started sharing about my own experiences with the LORD, HIS love and faithfulness in spite of me and the lady made this amazing remark that encouraged me so much. She stated, "I have heard people talking about GOD, but I have never heard anyone who talks like they actually know GOD." I trust that like you, my depth of intimacy will continue to grow in HIM but one of our keys is "Don't be Afraid."

END TIMES

HE replied: "Watch out that you are not deceived. For many will come in MY NAME, claiming, 'I am HE,' and, 'The time is near.' Do not follow them. When you hear of wars and revolutions, Do not be Frightened. These things must happen first, but the end will not come right away.

Luke 21:8, 9

The return of JESUS CHRIST is a prophetic reality just as HIS birth, death, and resurrection was a prophetic reality that came about. Many were unable to accept who JESUS CHRIST was during HIS earthly ministry because HE did not come as their minds perceived HE would come. As we look forward to HIS return in the 21st Century many Biblical scholars try to figure out when HIS return to earth will come even as it relates to when the rapture of the Church will take place. It always seems when man feels they have it all figured out the one thing we know is we probably don't in spite of all the prophetic words, but we will honor HIM and have eternity to thank HIM. In JESUS teaching to HIS disciples, HE shares events that will take place prior to HIS return to prepare HIS followers (you and I) for some signs that will take place before HE returns. JESUS in fact encourages us to recognize the signs and how we are to respond during these times that HE refers to. We see the faithfulness of the LORD preparing HIS people in advance as long as we look and recognize the signs.

As I examine Luke 21 and Matthew 24, which are referred to as signs of the end of the age, there is so much that is so deep, but the underlying issues raised are all based out of intimacy, trust and faith in our LORD. In these Chapter HE covers key points such as:

Don't be deceived

Wars and revolutions

Nations against nations

Kingdom against kingdom

Earthquakes, famines & pestilences

Betrayals

Jerusalem being surrounded

The end will not come right away

Signs from heaven

Delivered into synagogues

None to resist

Perish

Surrounded by enemies

Flee to the mountains

Time of punishment

Times of the Gentiles

Lift up your heads

Look to the fig tree

This generation

That day

The whole earth

Each day

Feast of unleavened Bread

Not a hair on your head

When JESUS came to the earth the first time the religious leaders of the day could not accept HIM, HIS teachings, HIS miracles, HIS ways, or HIS resurrection.   Before JESUS comes again (2ND time) HE has given HIS followers a clear picture of what will be taking place and with all due respect, none of us know when HE will return. In JESUS words Matthew 24:36 "No one knows about that day or hour, not even the angels of heaven, nor the SON, but only the FATHER." but just so we do not ignore the signs HE also gives HIS instructions: Matthew 24:42 "Therefore keep watch, because you do not know on what day your LORD will come."

What JESUS referenced in the noted scripture is that we are not to be deceived and in the 21st Century how often do we hear of the different cults and wayward teachings supposedly in the name of our LORD but contrary to the word of the LORD. What we do know is we are to be prepared and it is interesting that one of the first keys that HE gives is "Do not be Frightened.'

DISCIPLES

"All this I have spoken while still with you. But the COUNSELOR, the HOLY SPIRIT, whom the FATHER will send in MY NAME, will teach you all things and will remind you of everything I have said to you. Peace I leave with you; MY peace I give you. I do not give to you as the world gives. Do not let your hearts be troubled and Do not be Afraid." John 14:25-27

There are times when the LORD really wants to teach and reveal matters to us. At this particular time Judas made the decision to betray JESUS and had left HIM and his fellow disciples and we see JESUS teaching HIS disciples about trusting HIM, preparing a place for them, the oneness of the FATHER and the SON, the promise of the HOLY SPIRIT and obedience.

JESUS had shared with HIS disciples that HE would be leaving them soon and that where HE is going they can not come with HIM but that HE is going ahead of them to prepare a place for them. It is so easy for us, 2000 years later to wonder what the big deal was with the disciples. I am sure after HIS death and resurrection followed by HIS promise of the HOLY SPIRIT, which the disciples received at Pentecost that they too would wonder how they missed the obvious. Hindsight makes us all so smart. The question for us is what has HE shared with you or what is HE preparing for you that is either almost unbelievable or doesn't fully make sense?

How blessed we are that we have the precious HOLY SPIRIT now whom the FATHER sent in JESUS NAME. If the FATHER in agreement with the SON sent us the HOLY SPIRIT it is not only a good gift but also a necessary gift that we need to receive, welcome and walk in the fullness of. Our precious HOLY SPIRIT loves to teach us, loves to give revelation to us, loves to see the fruit of HIS SPIRIT being fulfilled through us, loves to release the gifts of the SPIRIT in us and through us loves to counsel and comfort, loves to have intimacy with us, loves it when we can be led by HIM, loves to honor the FATHER and glorify the SON, loves it when we serve the FATHER and SON and loves to fulfill destiny and inheritance in our lives.

The walk of faith requires faith because without faith it is impossible to please GOD. If you find yourself between a rock and a hard place, then receive the peace that passes all understanding that JESUS refers to and continue to grow in intimacy and love with the HOLY SPIRIT who will lead you in all truth and teach you all things. As the word says in 1 Corinthians 2:9-11 However, as it is written: "No eye has seen, no ear has heard, no mind has conceived what GOD has prepared for those who love HIM," but GOD has revealed it to us by HIS SPIRIT. The SPIRIT searches all things, even the deep things of GOD. For who among men knows the thoughts of a man except the man's spirit within him? In the same way no one knows the thoughts of GOD except the SPIRIT of GOD."

My wife Sandra and I were travelling in a foreign country and there was a delay of our plane leaving to return to Canada. We decided to browse in some stores to help kill the time. I must admit it is not one of my giftings. We walked into this particular store that Sandra felt led to go into and I noticed an unoccupied chair which I quickly occupied. While Sandra was browsing, I was approached by the Store Manager and we engaged in friendly conversation. The conversation quickly turned spiritual and he proudly told me of his eastern religion which was clearly not Christian but said that he knew of Christianity. He stressed his religion several times and all of a sudden the HOLY SPIRIT whispered to me "I have called this man to preach the Gospel of JESUS CHRIST to his own people." I was startled at the word but shared "The LORD JESUS CHRIST wants you to know that HE has called you to preach HIS Gospel to your own people." This man looked at me and started weeping and weeping. He stated that his religion was phoney, dead and hypocritical. He shared that since he was a small boy he had dreamed of preaching the gospel of JESUS CHRIST to his people just like Billy Graham did to the crowds even though he was not a Christian. He had never shared this dream and he knew that the only person that knew of this dream and calling was the

LORD JESUS. You can imagine the scene as this manager is on his knees praying to accept JESUS CHRIST as his personal SAVIOR. Sandra approached us with a sales lady who was already born again, subsequent tears, hugs and joy filled that store while angels in heaven were rejoicing.

In Chapter 14 of John there are a few words of comfort the LORD gives along with some "IF" conditions. Let's take a look at the "IF's": John 14: 7 "IF you really knew ME you would love ME, you would know my FATHER as well. From now on, you do know HIM and have seen HIM." and John 14:15 " IF you love ME, you will obey what I command." and John 14: 23 JESUS replied, IF anyone loves ME, he will obey MY teaching, MY FATHER will love him, and WE will come to him and make OUR home with him. Those "IF's" apply to not only the disciples but us as well. When JESUS is giving them comfort it is in these words: John 14:1 "Do not let your hearts be troubled. Trust in GOD: trust also in ME." and in our noted scripture where HE confirms the words, "Do not let your hearts be troubled and Do not be Afraid'"

GOD desires to be up to something in our lives and we need to recognize that is HIS love and way. Really get to know and love HIM so the words of JESUS are as relevant to you and me today as they were 2,000 years ago. "Do no let your hearts be troubled and Do not be Afraid." Watch what HE is about to do.

PILATE

The Jews insisted, "We have a law, and according to that law HE must die, because HE claimed to be the SON of GOD."
When Pilate heard this, he was even more Afraid.
John 19:7, 8

This scripture has been chosen as it reflects man's issues of dealing with man and the law regarding the truth of JESUS CHRIST and how compromise affects our lives.

As we know, the religious leaders of the day handed JESUS CHRIST over to Pilate, the Roman governor at the time to have HIM put to death. In the initial exchange between JESUS and Pilate, the conversation revolved around JESUS being King of the Jews and the Kingdom of GOD and ends with Pilate asking the question, "What is truth?" This simple question on the surface seems insignificant but if you examine who (and the position he holds) is asking the question, it gives us a better understanding of why the question. Scripture tells us to pray for those in Authority and we must understand that those in leadership, especially in politics are forever being used and abused with compromises. Conversely when you have power it is even easier to use and abuse it.

In fact, as you become comfortable with compromises everything can become very grey. Pilate asks the question of what charges they have against JESUS and then advises the religious leaders that there is no basis for the charges against JESUS and comes up with his compromise of releasing one prisoner. To Pilate's surprise, they do not choose JESUS as the prisoner to be released but instead they choose Barabbas even though he had taken place in a rebellion. The religious leaders at the time remind us of people who just love to argue about anything and everything and even end up even arguing with themselves. Pilate has JESUS flogged and figures that will satisfy the religious leaders but all he hears from them is 'Crucify', 'Crucify' and the reason they give is because JESUS claimed to be the SON of GOD. Verse 8 tells us that Pilate became even more Afraid and renews his conversation with JESUS about "power." Pilate tries to let JESUS know that as the Roman Governor he has power to either free HIM or to have HIM crucified. What an answer JESUS gives: John 19:11 JESUS answered, "You would have not power over ME if it were not given to you from above. Therefore, the one who handed me over to you is guilty of a greater sin."

Pilate is now being pulled and those are the last words that JESUS shares with Pilate. On one hand Pilate in spite of everything has a concern that JESUS could be the SON of GOD, King of the Jews and on the other hand, the people challenging Pilate that they have no king but Caesar and if he (Pilate) let's JESUS go, he (Pilate) is no friend of Caesar. Scripture states in Verse 16 that "Finally Pilate handed HIM over to them to be crucified." As often happens when spiritual compromises begin, the enemy does not want to let go of the open door he has on us and as we see in the word "finally" it becomes reality.

Let us realize that Pilate compromised his spirit of Fear for political purposes. We need to be so sensitive and aware of the little compromises that we make. The enemy is trying to put us into a corner and the decisions we make are never the right ones but are the compromised ones. In this particular case the normal Jewish custom would be for the stoning of JESUS but HIS death for us was to be by crucifixion to bear the curse for us. What love! What a SAVIOR! What a price to pay for us! How can we not be on our knees worshipping HIM with all our Heart? There are different kinds of Fear but as the word of GOD has taught us, "Do not be Afraid."

PAUL

But now I urge you to keep up your courage, because not one of you will be lost; only the ship will be destroyed. Last night an angel of the GOD whose I am and whom I serve stood beside me and said, "Do not be Afraid, Paul. You must stand trial before Caesar; and GOD has graciously given you the lives of all who sail with you.' So keep up your courage, men, for I have faith in GOD that it will happen just as HE told me.

Acts 27:22-25

Paul was one incredible man of GOD who in his Epistle letters would introduce himself as Paul, called to be an Apostle of JESUS CHRIST by the will of GOD. This same Paul was on a ship destined for Rome. This was not a cruise ship, and Paul was not a paid customer, rather he was a prisoner only because he had, as a Roman citizen appealed his case to Caesar, because in reality he had done nothing that deserved death or imprisonment.

Paul was charged because of his obvious faith in JESUS CHRIST and proclaiming the resurrection of JESUS CHRIST. Thus, the persecution and charges against him. The trip became a dangerous one because of a severe windstorm. Paul expressed his concern and gave his advice to the Centurion who did not listen to Paul, but rather to the pilot and the owner of the ship. It is one thing to address the crew of a boat if you have a position of authority, especially when you bring the things of GOD into the matter, but it is another when you are a prisoner and as a result, having little, if any credibility. It is important to re-affirm that Paul knew who he was in JESUS CHRIST and that gave him the authority. Being a prisoner was a purpose and process of our LORD for Paul, who eventually, upon reaching Rome, spent two years there preaching the Kingdom of GOD and taught about the LORD JESUS CHRIST. Paul's life was not his own and as followers of JESUS CHRIST, we claim our life is not as well. In any case, Paul addresses the crew, who by this time had given up all hope of being saved, with boldness that all of us should desire to have. There is nothing religious about what Paul stated; it was all personal to him:

GOD who I belong to

I serve GOD

GOD sent an angel

The angel gave me a message

GOD will protect your lives because you are travelling with me

What GOD says, HE will do

Because of all the above, have courage and don't look at the circumstances.

What did the angel say to Paul, about Paul?

Do not be Afraid

You must appear before Caesar

These men with you will not lose their lives

Isn't it clear how Paul brought his relationship with GOD into the lives of the crew? You can know that Paul really believed what he wrote in Romans 10:15b, when he states: As it is written, "How beautiful are the feet of those who bring Good

News!" It is also clear that the angel was instructed to ensure Paul the Apostle heard the words "Do not be Afraid" and everything flowed from that message.

Paul was a mighty man of GOD but on this occasion, even he had comfort from these words. Anyone who wants to self promote themselves as an Apostle should take Paul's description of an Apostle to heart as described in 1 Corinthians 4:9-13. 'For it seems to me that GOD has put us Apostles on display at the end of the procession, like men condemned to die in the arena. We have been made a spectacle to the whole universe, to angels as well as to men. We are fools for CHRIST, but you are so wise in CHRIST! We are weak, but you are strong! You are honoured, we are dishonoured! To this very hour we go hungry and thirsty, we are in rags, we are brutally treated, and we are homeless. We work hard with our own hands. When we are cursed, we bless; when are persecuted, we endure it; when we are slandered, we answer kindly. Up to this moment we have become the scum of the earth, the refuse of the world.'

If you ever have the opportunity to go to places like Corinth, Crete, Ephesus or Israel in the middle of the summer during a heat wave, it will make you appreciate how tough Paul was. Paul was a fearless man of GOD for the purposes and calling of his LORD. He was fully prepared to pay whatever price he needed to pay for the cause of his LORD. He had such a focus of walking in obedience to fulfill GOD'S purpose for his life. Out of his intimacy of love and relationship with JESUS, Paul knew his life was not his own but even Paul heard the words "Do not be Afraid."

PETER

Who is going to harm you if you are eager to do good? But even if you should suffer for what is right, you are blessed. "Do not Fear what they Fear; do not be Frightened." But in your hearts set apart CHRIST as LORD. Always be prepared to give an answer to everyone who asks you to give the reason for the hope that you have. But do this with gentleness and respect

1 Peter 3:13-15

As we examine the words written by the Apostle Peter, I cannot think of a better testimony that honours the transforming power of the HOLY SPIRIT in a person than in Peter. Let's remember this is the same Peter who cut off the right ear of a high priest when JESUS was being arrested, that denied knowing and being a follower of JESUS on three separate occasions, that was rebuked by JESUS when he told JESUS that HE was not going to wash Peter's feet, that he got out of the boat to walk on water, going up with JESUS when HE was transfigured offering to build shelters for Moses,

Elijah and JESUS, and the list goes on. All glory and honour to HIM for HIS transforming work in Peter's life. What is your testimony? And although different from Peter's think about it and don't deny your incredible testimony. It is important to recognize major events in the Apostle Peters life subsequent to the death and resurrection of JESUS CHRIST.

1. In John Chapter 21 we have to recognize the timing of this intimate conversation between JESUS and Peter by the Sea of Tiberias, that has taken place after Peter went to the empty tomb but could not fully understand the resurrection. After JESUS had appeared to Peter and the other disciples, Peter, the fisherman decided to go fishing and several of the disciples went with him. They spent the whole night catching nothing and along comes JESUS telling them to throw the net on the other side of the boat and their catch was 153 large fish. You have to feel for Peter the fisherman but put yourself in Peter's position, and what he felt like carrying all the

shame, humility, unworthiness, brokenness, and guilt. After breakfast, JESUS resurrects Peter's calling and purpose in the most beautiful, challenging and sensitive way. You might feel as Peter felt but allow the HOLY SPIRIT to speak destiny and resurrection into your life as well. Let's take a minute and read this exchange. John 21: 15-17 When they had finished eating, JESUS said to Simon Peter, "Simon son of John, do you truly love me more than these?" "Yes LORD," he said, "you know that I love you." JESUS said, "Feed my lambs." Again, JESUS said, "Simon son of John, do you truly love me?" He answered, "Yes, LORD, you know that I love you." JESUS said, "Take care of my sheep." The third time HE said to him, Simon son of John, do you love me?" Peter was hurt because JESUS asked him the third time, "Do you love me?" He said, "LORD, you know all things: you know that I love YOU." JESUS said, Feed my sheep." JESUS goes on to explain to Peter the kind of death

Peter would experience in glorifying GOD and finishes with, "Follow me." We need to be encouraged in our own faith in following JESUS, allowing HIM to talk to us as HE did to Peter.

2. As noted in Acts Chapter 2 Peter along with the other Apostles on the day of Pentecost received the promise from JESUS of the HOLY SPIRIT and became one of the leading Apostles in the New Covenant Church. Receiving the fullness of the HOLY SPIRIT should be a daily desire of all of us. Just read the sermon of Peter to the crowd in Jerusalem in Acts 2 and be encouraged. We need to realize the out pouring of HIS SPIRIT on Pentecost changed not only the Apostles but the history of the world. Although over history there have been pockets of revivals we can look forward to HIS promise in the book of Joel of HIS pouring out of HIS SPIRIT in the last days.

3. As we know the initial followers of JESUS believed the Gospel was for the Jewish people and not the Gentiles until Paul has his revelation from the HOLY SPIRIT and then Peter who was deeply respected as a Apostle and Father of the faith had his experience in Acts 10 where the HOLY SPIRIT instructed Peter to go to Cornelius home and while there, it was revealed by the SPIRIT to Peter that the Gospel of JESUS CHRIST was for both Jew and Gentile. Peter subsequently shared with the other Apostles what had been revealed to him and it was a change of mindset for all of them.

4. Carefully read the two Epistles of Peter and as you examine them reflect on how this mighty Apostle was truly empowered to become the man of GOD he became and marvel at how his faith was developed as he walked in obedience, faith and love. He imparts such wisdom and counsel for all of us.

With that as a backdrop, when we read Peter's words to us about how to conduct our lives it is important to recognize the words, "Do not Fear what they Fear, Do not be Frightened." Just take time and praise our GOD for HE is good.

REVELATION GIVEN TO JOHN

When I saw HIM, I fell at HIS feet as though dead. Then HE placed HIS right hand on me and said: "Do not be Afraid. I am the FIRST and the LAST. I am the LIVING ONE; I was dead, and behold I am alive for ever and ever! And I hold the keys of death and Hades."
Revelation 1:17, 18

The Apostle John while on the Island of Patmos for the cause of CHRIST is in the SPIRIT having this supernatural visitation and is instructed to write on a scroll what he has seen and to send it to the seven churches. A key for any revelation from our GOD is we must be in the SPIRIT. John hears a loud voice like a trumpet and John states he sees someone "like a SON of MAN" and falls at his feet. Who would not want the same experience that John had and notice the words of comfort for John, "Do not be Afraid."? To fully understand the words of comfort to John we need to read what John saw and place yourself in John's place and ask yourself how you would have reacted? Revelation 1: 12-16

I turned around to see the voice that was speaking to me. And when I turned, I saw seven golden lampstands, and among the lampstands was someone "like a SON of MAN", dressed in a robe reaching down to HIS feet and with a golden sash around HIS chest. HIS head and hair were white like wool as white as snow, and HIS eyes were like blazing fire. HIS feet were like bronze glowing in a furnace, and HIS voice was like the sound of rushing waters. In HIS right hand HE held seven stars, and out of HIS mouth came a sharp double-edged sword. HIS face was like the sun shining in all its brilliance.

I hope we can understand why John fell at HIS feet as though dead. Out of total submission, reverence, awe, worship and love was John's reaction. How would we have reacted? It's like the question "if JESUS walked into our Church service today how would we all react?"

There is such a blessing from the LORD for us in Revelation 1: 3 "Blessed is the one who reads the words of this prophecy and blessed are those who hear it and take it to heart, what is written in it, because the time is near. "

John had not only a message from the LORD for the seven churches, but he also recorded what he saw later in detail. It is well worth it to read the letters to the seven Churches as a Church body and determine what type of Church you are and then determine what the LORD is saying to your Church for the changes HE desires to be made.

The book of Revelation is some book to write and what an honour and responsibility given to John. As the last chapter in this book, I believe it is also fitting for us to understand that again we have one of JESUS closest disciples who has such an experience that before he can begin the task in front of him, those familiar words of comfort are spoken to him.

We (the church) are about to enter into a time, when great revelation will be given to us and we are going to be asked to do some amazing things. What the Apostle John encountered is unique but for some of us taking a new job is unique, whether or when to have a child, the right career studies, getting married, whether to buy a house, go to missions, speak to the Nations, etc. What is important is for us to understand the signs and times, have ears to hear and eyes to see and like the Apostle John to be '"in the SPIRIT."

This Chapter of the book "Don't be Afraid" is not to do a synopsis of the book of Revelation but to understand John's experience of falling down in reverence at HIS feet and realizing HE is coming soon for us. As you read Chapter 22, which is the last chapter in the Bible, you will see these words of JESUS: Revelation 22: 12-13 "Behold, I am coming soon! MY reward is with ME, and I will give to everyone according to what he has done. I am the ALPHA and OMEGA, the FIRST and the LAST, the BEGINNING and the END." Remember the words given to John, "Do not be Afraid."

40281793R00137

Made in the USA
Middletown, DE
26 March 2019